The Rural Solution

For Deirdre.

The Rural SOLUTION

Modern Catholic Voices on Going "Back to the Land"

Traditionalist Press
The true friends of the people are neither revolutionaries nor innovators: they are traditionalists. –St. Pius X
2003 County Longford, Ireland

The Rural Solution.

The Editors wish to extend their kindest thanks to the Most Rev. Richard Williamson, Dr. Peter Chojnowski, and Mr. Christopher McCann, for gracious permission to include their original works as part of this new collection. We wish also to gratefully acknowledge the permission granted by the Editor of the Angelus Press to include herein articles originally published in *Integrity Magazine*.

ISBN: 0-9545632-0-4

Published by The Traditionalist Press.

British Library Cataloguing in Publication Data

The rural solution : modern Catholic voices on going "back to the land"
1.Sociology, Rural - Religious aspects - Catholic Church
2.Sociology, Rural - Philosophy 3.Economics - Religious
aspects - Catholic Church 4.Catholics - Religious life
I.Williamson, Richard II.Palin, David
307.7'2'08822

ISBN 0954563204

For more information about this or other titles, please contact:

The Traditionalist Press
Box 1
Moyne
County Longford
Ireland

Printed in the United States of America.

Contents

"One hope for relief in the universal misery of the present lies in the reversal of the policy which produced the factory and the factory system. This reversal without depriving men of the benefits of industrial progress, would reinstate them as independent home owners in rural communities. Such a change in the living conditions of millions of people would be a revolution, but some radical adjustment in restoring the balance between rural and urban population is imperative if our country is to survive and if our civilization is not to disappear."

—Bishops of the Administrative
Committees of the U.S. National
Catholic Welfare Conference
April 26, 1933

Introduction

When you hear that some people are "going back to the land", what kind of images come to mind?

Perhaps it is the Great Unwashed: the scruffy, long-haired, hashish-smoking drop-out who retires to a commune in the country where illegal substances and unrestricted fornication provide the background to life, and which is usually paid for by government handouts in the form of welfare extracted from unwilling but hard-working taxpayers.

Perhaps it is the survivalist: that over-earnest patriot who moves his family – lock, stock and barrel – to a homestead in the wilderness where a non-bumpy road is regarded as the "contamination of civilization", where the nearest neighbour is about fifty miles away, and where the holed-up family waits anxiously for *Red Dawn* – the arrival of the Commie hordes.

Perhaps it is the man who was, until recently, something "big" at the Stock Exchange or at "Goldman, Goldberg and Goldblatt: Investment Analysts and Financial Consultants"; but who, out of the blue, sells his plush city residence and moves to the wide-open countryside. Being a sober kind of gentleman, he has been instrumental in keeping the rat race of modern society going, but has now decided to drop out – having made his "stash" from the relentless exploitation of others – and live out his days in Arcadian bliss.

There are, of course, any number of images that come to mind when the subject is the return to the land, but *whatever* image it is, it is one that is exceptional, eccentric, expedient, or plain crazy. Yet it ought not be any of those, for a return to the land is, above all, a call to the ordinary, decent citizen to seek sanity and salvation. That it does not appear a call to the ordinary, but to the *extraordinary*, is really a measure and judgement of the times – times which are intellectually diseased, culturally decadent and spiritually moribund.

It is hardly necessary to be a Professor of History at an accredited university to know that the bulk of people living on the land, living off the land, has been the general condition of humanity throughout the centuries. It is not something that was merely true in the ancient world, or only in the medieval world, but something that remained the case in most European countries up until the bloody and futile catastrophe known as World War I. The peasant and the farmer were the norm in all the great civilizations, and their contribution to life in all its aspects was perfectly complemented by that smaller, but important, class of men who constituted the Crafts. They were in a mutually satisfactory and symbiotic relationship: the Glove that graced the Hand, the Poem that expressed the Principle, the Song that was born of Love.

It is, therefore, truly a sign of the times that a return to the land, a return to the norm, a return to humanity's true home, is regarded as out of the ordinary – even "weird" to use the language of "street-wise" man. That non-Catholics should find a return to the land "weird" is bad enough, a sufficient cause for weeping; but that Catholics should feel likewise is nothing less than scandalous, perhaps even blasphemous, for it clearly betrays a gross misunderstanding of one aspect of the life of the Holy Family. It is little remembered by the mass of Catholics that Christ's life was full of symbolism, and one area, in particular, where the significance of the symbolism has been lost in our time is in the choice of His birth place. Does it not strike the reader as peculiar that Christ was *not* born in the great city of Jerusalem, or the capital of the ancient world, Rome? These were the sites of spiritual and political *power*, and yet Christ is born in Bethlehem and raised in Nazareth. Neither is a megalopolis nor even a city. Each is modest, ordinary, humble. They are the abodes of simple peasants and craftsmen; not of Princes and Captains of Industry. Even the mildest of reflections would reveal that Christ's lesson was plain and simple: *"I choose the Peasant and Craftsman and the Land because that is the Will of My Father".* Why? Because life on the land, as peasant or craftsman, means contact with Nature – and the author of Nature is thus apprehended directly, daily and, one might even say, almost instinctively. The Art – *Creation* – and the Artist – *God* – are correlated so that even the simpleton can see the truth, but in the city the Art is deformed or destroyed, and the Artist is obscured or obliterated in the mind's eye of millions of men and women.

This position on the Land and its centrality to Civilization and to Catholicism is not a matter of merely private opinion. It is an expression of the mind of the Church. Fr. Vincent McNabb, O.P., for example, wrote the following in *The Church and the Land*: "If there is one truth more than another which life and thought have made us admit, against our prejudices and even against our will, it is that there is little hope of saving civilization or religion except by the return of contemplatives to the land!"

In the Joint Pastoral Letter of the Hierarchy of Quebec issued in November, 1937, and entitled "On the Rural Problem", their Lordships stated the following boldly:

> Dare We then affirm that rural life is the normal state for the masses? In a century such as ours, with its various allurements and demands, when the farmers, in most countries, have been uprooted from the soil and concentrated in the cities, it is unwelcome advice, it seems, to urge so many new city-dwellers to return to the land, or even to induce those who still dwell upon it to remain there. We are willing to admit that rural life must not henceforth be regarded in terms of the isolation and hardships that so long weighed upon our farmers, who, like the rest of us, are entitled to profit by scientific improvements and inventions. Nevertheless, in spite of the developments of mechanical production, the basic industry must ever remain that of obtaining from the soil the daily bread of humanity.

The statement is one rich in both content and vision. It says categorically that life on the land is the norm, and it is so because without such life there is no daily bread; that is to say, if the land is not worked, we *starve*. It draws attention to the phoney nature of city life, with its neon lights and its "conveniences". It makes clear that genuine advances in science and technology – while properly subordinated to a sane, agrarian order – *must* be used to the benefit of the farmer in order that his lot might be ameliorated greatly, thus destroying the media-induced lie that Holy Church opposes genuine Progress, and demonstrating rather Her maternal love for the tillers of the soil. For an institution that is reputedly "out of date" and "out of touch", the Church is remarkably in tune with the interests and sympathies of humanity!

Now it might be argued – tendentiously – that the return to the land is something vouchsafed to a particular kind of Catholic; that it is a legitimate vocation, if a minority one. But is that really so? Granted that, in a period of immense societal decadence, it will be missionaries "possessed" by a vision, by a vocation, who will lead the return to the land and to sanity, it remains nonetheless the case that the call is made to the majority of Catholics – not to the mere enthusiastic few. Why? Because life on the Land gives the Faith roots in rich soil, whilst life in the City for the Faith is sterile and ultimately destructive of the Catholic Church. This is seen not merely in the decline of city parishes, but even in the decline of the numbers of Catholics born. The point was eloquently made by our own Fr. McNabb, and confirmed as well by the work of the Americans' "National Catholic Rural Life Conference". There can be no argument on this matter, other than by sophists who play games with statistics to the detriment of reality.

It has also been argued – rather perversely – that a return to the land by Catholics would be a sign of retreat, if not of outright defeat, and that it corresponds to a neglect of their apostolic duties towards non-Catholic city dwellers. This kind of argument can only be maintained by those who have a very superficial grasp of Catholic Social Teaching generally, and of a Return to the Land specifically. It ignores a number of important points which radically transform the discussion. *Firstly*, "the advance" towards the city was not the by-product of free will, rather it was done through legal trickery and persecution. This being so, the position held in the city is *not* of its nature a Catholic one at all; thus, giving it away involves no loss whatever for Catholics and for Catholicism. Indirectly it is even a gain, for it permits Catholics to position themselves – literally and figuratively – on their natural terrain! *Secondly*, and perhaps more pertinently, a retreat is *not* a defeat. There have been any number of occasions in history when a body of people have been on the point of being overwhelmed by superior forces, who have chosen to retreat and regroup – and whose decision to do so allowed them not only to survive but to go on to victory. A return to the land would be a sign of understanding and intelligence, for it would demonstrate that Catholics had at long last grasped reality: the world hates us because we possess the Truth, and it will not rest until we cease to exist. If we have to retreat, therefore, in order to prepare the counter-attack, so be it! *Finally*, there is the simple fact that the most *truly persuasive* apostolate of all is the *living of an integral, Catholic life on the land.* Actions, it is said, speak louder than words, and if that is so then the move to a wholesome, natural, and Catholic way of life is tantamount to preaching the Good News from the housetops.

This call to the land is not restricted to Catholics imbued with zeal for the subject. The land, its appeal, its centrality to man's existence is so elemental, so ingrained – one might even exaggerate (on the right side of the argument) by claiming that it is almost genetically encoded in human beings – that it finds its advocates even outside the visible confines of Holy Church. Thus, H. J. Massingham, the Anglican author and ideologue, writes eloquently in *The Tree of Life*:

> If the village birth and upbringing of Christ be mythological, the record of His mission is unaccountable. His journeyings were so completely those of a countryman, his associations so obviously rural, his followers so clearly drawn from small market towns and villages and his own concrete and pictorial methods of expression so fundamentally a peasant speech transfigured that, if He was not actually born in a manger and visited by shepherds, it would have been necessary to have invented that He did. His debt to his native soil was indeed far more explicitly expressed than Shakespeare's, on whose work the stamp of country England was incomparably more sharply and indelibly impressed than it was on any of his contemporary dramatists. Shakespeare actually spent the best years of his life in the capital; Christ never entered it except on seasonal occasions and to mark the apotheosis of his earthly visitation.

It is an historical fact that England was the first country in Europe which began the process of destroying the peasantry, and herding the men, women and children into the cities. It was done by a malevolent and fanatical few driven by a profound hatred of Catholicism and, implicitly, by a profound hatred of their fellowmen. It was one of the main fruits – putrid in the extreme – of the so-called Protestant Reformation which, as it progressed, had less and less to do with religious or theological arguments, and more and more to do with creating a society where the rich and the ruthless could prosper at the expense of the Common Man. The Statute of Frauds, coupled with the Enclosures movement, "relieved" the Church of much of her lands and provided for the widespread "legal" confiscation of peasant property. The result is, of course, that England has not had a living peasantry – or yeomanry, if you prefer – for over four centuries. If ever a country has been cut off from the normal routine of life on the land, it is England. And yet we find in a recent survey carried out in England by a major polling agency that a little over half of the interviewees remarked that if they had the opportunity, they would willingly return to the land. Four centuries of flight to the city, four centuries of drumming into people that the city is "where it's at", four centuries of "educating" people that farming is for "dumb folk" and something to be looked down upon – and yet still more than 50% of the English would go back to the land if it were made possible.

The survey does not tell us *why* so many would be willing to tread the path of difficulty towards the land, but we can hazard intelligent guesses.

The first is clearly related to the environment. Whether politicians admit it or not, the fact is the city is now home to countless scenes of urban deprivation: rampant criminality; a drug culture that spreads daily; an environment where traffic jams, polluted air and endless noise are the norm; a juvenile delinquency that has ceased being mere boredom and pushes the boundaries of nihilism ever-further backwards; the loss of any sense of community spirit as a myriad of alien cultures, languages and religions are squeezed into high-rise flats and sprawling, soulless housing estates; endless commuting that strains the very nerves of a man, and pushes stress levels off the scale; a myriad of social, economic and psychological problems so complex and so interrelated that only a government of talented, even exceptional, men with real power and authority could hope to sort them out.

It is becoming obvious to observers with any kind of sensitivity that the current direction of modern society is going to end in catastrophe. The stresses and strains are more than the human frame can bear – especially when that frame is in most cases devoid of any real contact with God. A man can, for a period, stand a war, military or psychological, when he has the presence of God with him, intimately and daily; but when it is an open-ended war without the presence of God, it is absolutely inevitable that a man will crack under the strain. And what is true of an individual man is as true, if not more so, of a society.

Wherever one looks, one sees all kinds of attempts to reclaim "normality". Rambling, gardening, herb growing, country visits, the study of the arts and crafts and all the rest of it. There is clearly a movement, a tendency at foot which, though not specific, is drifting, here and there, in the right direction. People know that there are problems, and they are seeking answers. It is because they don't possess the Catholic faith in too many cases, or are wholly ignorant of the claims of the Church, that they don't respond in a Catholic way. But the rise of all kinds of movements, sects and even strange religions is a testimony to the thirst that exists in our world for the Truth. Yet it is equally true that modernist "Catholics" are too antiquated in their thinking and methodology to recognize this fact and act accordingly. More and more people are recognizing – at least subconsciously – that relativism (which is what Modernism is at heart) is not the answer. The answer to problems, especially human and spiritual problems, is *certitude*. A man will die for an absolute truth; he will not so much as cross the road for a relative one.

The desire to escape social alienation, social dependency, bureaucratic interference, consumerism, the dead-hand of crass materialism, the inanities of “sex, drugs and rock ‘n’ roll”, the endless rushing to and fro in the search for...what? – this is all evident to the intelligent eye. But if people are seeking a spiritual renewal, a desire to be self-sufficient, a way that gives hope, why are so few actually returning to the land? If something like 50% of England’s urban population want to move to the land, why don’t they?

The answers are many and varied, and this Introduction does not even pretend to furnish more than the barest inklings of an answer, but at the end of the day the fundamental question is psychological and spiritual.

We have become habituated to listening to “the experts”. It is they who in large part direct the movement of our decrepit society through exclusive interviews in “quality” newspapers, through appearing on “serious” documentaries or special TV news features, through standing shoulder to shoulder with the movers and shakers of the power elite. Yet it remains in many cases – too many in fact – that their expertise is more than questionable both in its content and in its relevance. They can argue whether drug A or drug B is more efficacious – but they never see the possibility that perhaps both A and B are unnecessary or unacceptable. They can argue whether Monetarism or Deficit Spending is the superior financial policy – without ever seeing that neither makes any sense in the world of real – as opposed to virtual – economics.

Experts being thus the backdrop to our society, it is not surprising that many people pick up their notions from the “white noise” of discussion that passes for intellectual debate. The experts tell us that we don’t need more people on the land, but *fewer.* The experts tell us that rugged self-sufficiency and independence is now passé, since we all live in the "global village". The experts tell us that as long as consumption is rising, that credit is readily available, and that people can shop 7 days a week, day or night, then society is in a healthy condition. These arguments and many variations on such themes have, subconsciously, convinced many folk, desirous of another way of life, that they are seeking to "turn the clock back", that they are "out of step" with the modern world; that they are, in a word, *plain silly*.

It is when one sees that this is the very real situation which confronts us that we come to appreciate why people do not act upon their desires. *They fear.* They fear what the family and neighbours will think. They fear that the undertaking is too much for them. They fear failure. They fear that they don't have the talents and the skills required. They fear that they will end up penniless and in dire poverty. They fear...everything that under-active or over-active minds can throw up.

Yet such people never seem to balance up this debit sheet of Fear with another debit sheet of Fear that cancels out the first. Do they not fear the crime of the city streets? Do they not fear for their mental and physical health in atmospheres that are becoming evermore toxic? Do they not fear for the safety of their children? Do they not fear for their property in the face of widespread robbery? Do they not fear the letter from the company that tells them that they are out of a job?

Seen in this light, one sees immediately that modern people are living in *a climate of fear.* The only difference between fear of moving to the land and fear of living in the city is that the former offers the possibility of attaining a real quality of life, and passing it on to future generations, whilst the latter is, in the majority of cases, truly a dead end road. The fears, therefore, are *not* equal; the fear of returning to the land is obviously the lesser fear, and it is the one lined with hope. But since fear remains the primary obstacle to returning to the land, the obvious answer is that moral courage must be summoned up – a courage more difficult to possess than its merely physical counterpart. Then it only remains to look reality in the face, calculate the odds (for the situation of each family will differ), and then trust in the Providence of Almighty God.

Once this moral deficiency is overcome, everything else falls into place. Worries about jobs and income will give way to the awareness that there are similar jobs in the country, or even new enterprises to start up; that a move might be a perfect opportunity to escape the 9 a.m. to 5 p.m. rate race. Fears about lack of friends and contacts nearby will disappear in light of the fact that people in the countryside need one another – for car breakdowns, for snow on the road or whatever – and that connections *always* come with time. Concerns about "making it" as a farmer will come to be understood as valid *only* with the assumption that everyone *has to be* a farmer. There are plenty of alternatives, such as getting one acre of land and becoming a smallholder; buying merely half an acre and working part-time in a pub, with a local business, making pottery, writing books, painting houses, etc. The move to the land can be graduated to fit every kind of person and every kind of circumstance. And the fear of lacking the right kinds of skills to live on the land are easily alleviated by checking out the evening courses offered by the local college on the basics of whatever might be necessary: carpentry, electrics, plumbing, horticulture, and so on; or taking advantage of the opportunities afforded by any number of volunteer associations that offer weekend courses on all kinds of subjects from gardening to horse maintenance, that sell myriads of books on similar topics, and that can advise, guide, and train on all the aspects involved in the return to the land. With these simple facts in mind, it becomes clear that those who feel alone only do so because they *have not bothered* to find out just how much help is out there, and how varied the possibilities are for a successful return to the land.

Besides – are the many obstacles that litter the road that returns to the land any more dangerous than those along the road that leads to the worship of Mammon, a road which wears down bodies, deadens minds, and ultimately kills souls?

This book, then, is no more than an introduction to the idea of a return to the land. Reading it involves no commitments, but it may lead to an awareness of possibilities beyond the dreams of some Hollywood fantasy. It will not answer all questions by any means; but it will provide a good background in the matter, and offer at least "a feel" for the thing. It will not indicate exactly *what* should be done or *why*, but it will reveal what others have done and why they did it – and how they might be emulated, while adapting everything to particular circumstances and necessities. Above all, the book makes a persuasive case that living in the countryside is the most beneficial way to live for one who wishes to live an *authentic* and *integral* Catholicism. No one is alone who lives in the presence of Almighty God. No one who sincerely loves our Blessed Saviour would wish not to follow His rule in their lives. No one who is sincere in their Faith can afford not to read this book, reflect upon it, deepen their study of the subject, and then decide whether they can or cannot "take up their Cross and follow Me". For those who don't like where they are and what they are doing, we offer the following: *change* the circumstances of your situation. It might be hard. It might involve real sacrifice and renunciation, but then doesn't everything of importance require this? The choice may be hard, it may be difficult; but thanks to your God-given free will, *the choice is yours.*

The Traditionalist Press
June 29, 2003
Feast of Ss. Peter and Paul

Ruralism Versus Urbanism

by Bishop Richard Williamson

Q. Surely you are not attacking *cities,* which have always been centres of Catholic civilization and culture? St. Paul's Letters are all addressed to early churches in cities (Rome, Corinth, etc.). Medieval Cathedrals were all built in cities.

A. Correct. But industrialization, in particular the motor-car, changed radically the structure of cities, and the mentality of city-dwellers. For instance the people who had socialized and the children who had played in the city streets were chased off them by the motor-car. Similarly, as long as the country outweighed the cities, city-dwellers shared more or less of the country-men's common sense (e.g., you cannot fool with day or night, winter or summer), but as soon as industrialism enabled the cities to outweigh the country then that common sense began to be worn away (e.g., with electricity and central heating we can change night and winter). The modern city and suburbs easily erode this natural sense of there being a nature of things. Now without nature, where is grace?

Q. But the suburbs, like television, are merely neutral, and can be used for good or bad. The problem is sin. Attack sin, not suburbs!

A. It is precisely to attack sin that one attacks modern suburbs, because their way of life favours sin. Their softness and comfort favour sensuality (Second Sorrowful Mystery). The anti-socialness and independence of their way of life favour pride (Third Sorrowful Mystery). True, television is in theory neutral, but not in practice. As installed in the (suburban or modern city) home, it strongly tends to be misused, discombobulating mind, will, the sense of reality, activeness, humanness, and family. Similarly the suburbs in practice strongly tend to discombobulate human beings. Listen to the Rock musicians, voice of now two alienated generations (1960's to 1990's). This alienation cannot go on.

Q. But priests (and dinosaur bishops) should be attacking sin, which is the heart of the problem, and not suburbs, which are obviously not the heart of the problem.

A. Granted, of course, sin is the real problem. But if a child complains of its shoes hurting, is it foolish to point out that it has put the right shoe on the left foot, and vice versa? If Catholics complain of finding it very difficult to lead Catholic lives, is it foolish for priests to point out where they are not realizing that the whole context of their lives is carrying them towards pride and sensuality?

Q. What do you mean by "a context carrying towards sin"? Sins are committed by free choice, not by context!

A. Yes, but contexts can exert more or less pressure on free choice, which is why many of them are branded as "occasions of sin," which a Catholic must avoid.

Q. Then you are saying that modern suburbs are an occasion of sin? Ridiculous!

A. Let us take a different example. A car radio is, as such, not the best *context* for listening to classical music, because I am distracted by driving, I am purely passive to the music being played, I am by my "Seek" or "Scan" buttons master of the Great Masters, to replace them at will with umpteen Rock stations. Now I *can* listen to classical music on a car radio. But the context of attending a live concert is much better, where I am neither distracted, nor purely passive, nor master of the Masters by the push of a button. Similarly I can lead a Catholic life in the motor-car suburbs, but the whole context is man-made, man-centred, man-controlled. It is a *context* that shuts out God, making Him not impossible, but rather more difficult, to reach. Contexts count!

Q. You just do not like anything new.

A. Much wiser (Prov. XXII, 28) to like nothing new than to like nothing old, which is the condition and conditioning of modern man! But anything new that will help me to save my soul, like a new set of officials in Rome, truly Catholic, I will grab with both hands! A truly renewed Catholic Church, a new truly Christian World Order, yes please!

Q. But time passes, and things change. It is no use lamenting the "good old days."

A. There is no question of lamenting the good old yesterdays, only of judging correctly our present todays, in order to save as many souls as possible tomorrow. Of course time passes and things change. That is exactly why we must think about what time has brought us to now so that we can make things now change for the better. Otherwise they will go on changing for the worse. Change is inevitable, but God requires of us to direct that change in the direction of His will.

Q. But people have always praised times past as though they were better. Which strongly suggests that they were not really better at all.

A. The arguments for the Reign of Christ the King having – broadly – deteriorated for the last 700 years are clear and convincing. A car without brakes can free-wheel down a hill without crashing for a certain length of time, but finally it must crash. To the remains of Christendom in the 20th century, God sent three major warnings – World Wars I and II, and Vatican II. But still mankind is free-wheeling down-hill, and faster than ever.

Q. But country people are now as full of drugs and vices as city or suburban people.

A. Probably not quite, but that is much more true today than yesterday, precisely because the motor-car with all its pomps and all its works has overtaken the country. When Our Lady (allegedly) appeared in the mountain village of Garabandal in Northern Spain in the early 1960's, it was still an isolated mountain village. Now it is just an outrider of the nearest town.

Q. As for the American countryside, or heartland, it is full of Protestants, the farms are laid out in an anti-social way, and life is led there in a manner downright selfish.

A. As December's letter said, Protestantism is the heart of the problem of "suburbanism," so that to attack the symptom of suburbanism amounts to a way of alerting Catholics to how the disease of Protestantism *is most likely infecting them without their realizing it.* To be Catholic is, in itself, far more important than to live in the country, but, circumstantially, not living in the country can incline many Catholics to cease being Catholic at all. Accordingly, let any Catholic think twice before he moves away from the Mass to be in the country, and let him think thrice before moving into the country to recreate suburbs there, or to rejoin an industrialized, mechanized, anti-socialized way of life.

Q. Yes, we Catholics are not Amish!

A. By the Truth of our supernatural religion, no. But does that mean that there is nothing in their natural way of life from which we could profit by imitating? Not necessarily. There is "method in their madness." To live on the land is not the same as to live off the land.

Q. OK, OK! Supposing I do move into the country, close enough to get to Mass each day, with time enough to recite the Rosary each day, and on too few acres to get sucked into industrial farming. What then?

A. First, let no suburbanite pretend that the move back into the country is easy. Farming is a hard way of life, which is precisely why many people in the 20th century left the land for the cities. Cows take no holidays, they must be milked every day, which includes at dawn in the dead of winter! But "no sweat, no sweet." In the hardness of the life lies its salutary discipline, for youngsters and oldsters. If people had stayed on the land, Communism could never have arisen. Who would dream of going on strike against land, animals or weather? Conclusion: in order to achieve what you would have moved to the country to achieve, do not expect, and do not re-construct, the easy life for yourselves. “In suffering is learning.” Secondly, proximity to the Mass would be a crucial part of your move into the country, not only because of our Sunday duty and absolute need of the sacraments to save our souls, but also because of the *Catholic's need of community.* If Catholics fled the modern city or suburbs because of that whole context damaging to the Faith, it would not be worth fleeing into a Protestant context of isolated and individualistic country life, where there would be no Catholic families for miles around. In the early Middle Ages (500–1000 AD), the villages, towns, cities of Christendom formed around a monastery or church.

Q. But in the Middle Ages the altars of the Catholic Church were rather more stable than they are in today's crisis of the Church!

A. As we look back in time, it may seem so, but at that time amidst the ruins of the Roman empire and the threat of barbarian invasions, the altars may in fact have seemed hardly more stable than they do today. At some point God requires of us to take reasonable risks and to trust in Him for the rest.

Q. So I flee the suburbs and I re-locate in the country within striking distance of a group of Catholics where there is the Mass. What will I have achieved positively?

A. In the country, much more of the environment is God-made, or natural, instead of man-made, or artificial. Every creature of God speaks directly of God, if one has ears to listen.

So if one moved into the country, one should not make the move too humanly abrupt, with too many sudden changes, because the temptation might then be to come racing back to the good old suburbs one is used to. On the other hand one should envisage leaving behind, little by little, more and more of those artificialities which are the pride and consolation of suburbanites, and which fill the glossy colour catalogues stuffing our mail-boxes. Life in the country should simplify, and as it did so, the important things in life would come back into view, presently blocked out by multiple artificial distractions.

Q. But no museums, no concerts, no culture – just the beauties of Nature? How boring!

A. Moving into the country would require a period of adaptation, to survive which I would need to have well *thought out* why I had moved into the country in the first place. But if I had thought it through, I would stand a good chance of adapting successfully. For instance, in the cities, museums have constantly to make up new exhibitions from the same old artists, or else patronize the modern anti-artists. In the country, no two sunsets or sunrises are exactly the same, and each one is a fresh masterpiece painted in moving techno-colour, but of course one must have eyes to see. Similarly concert-halls have to go round and around the same favourite pieces of the classical composers, or else descend into the bear-pit of "modern music," whereas in the country each dawn-chorus of bird-song is a new symphony conducted by our Maker, but concert-hall ears have to be adjusted to hear it. (In one sense, the museums and concerts died some time ago.)

Q. But life in the country would be boring!

A. The adults would have to adjust, for sure, and the older children, but the younger children should take to country life like ducks to water. Most parents can see how much more healthy it would be for their children to grow up in the country, only circumstances of all kinds prevent them from thinking that they could make the move.

Q. What is the advantage for children?

A. Fresh air. Freedom to play outside. Manual labor, apt to teach discipline and responsibility. The handling of live animals for which children have a God-given affinity, and which by their God-given nature can teach many lessons of life that no machines can teach. For instance, what child born and bred in between stallions and mares, bulls and cows, cocks and hens, is ever going to buy into the absurdity that there is no difference between males and females? Dare I say that the animals *without* reason will have taught the child a significant part of the difference between males and females that *have* reason?

Q. But all of these advantages of country life are situated on the merely natural level. It is grace, or supernature, that counts for salvation!

A. Of course, but grace builds on nature. Grace does heal nature, but it does not violate it. Grace works against sin, but it works with nature. That is why a wise education works with grace and nature in tandem. The problem with the ever-increasing artificiality of suburban life is that nature is being so shattered that grace has nothing left to work with. The total suburban context makes stony ground on which the seed of grace has little chance. That is a major reason why so many pious suburban parents see their teenagers become disinterested in the Catholic religion. *Grace and nature, as presented to the teenagers, just do not integrate or fit one another.*

Two Pigs and a Cow

by Christopher McCann

Since the advent of the Industrial Revolution there has been an incessant worldwide influx of people into cities and industrial manufacturing. This transition has not been without its share of those who point out the material abuses, particularly the denial of the right to organize trade unions, unemployment, inhumane living and working conditions, low wages, interminable hours of work, and exploitation of all sorts. But there is a much more serious and more elusive problem with urban industrial life and it is spiritual in nature. I shall call it alienation.

This is not alienation as the Marxist sees it, which is an umbrella term for various economic theories such as alienation of need, alienation of useful labor and alienation of use-values which supposedly prove that for one man to work for another is an essentially unjust relationship. No, a Catholic understanding of a different alienation will unfold in this article based on the assumption that God created man to interact in harmony with the rest of creation and that this harmonious interaction was damaged by original sin but not destroyed by it. Thus alienation is in the sense of "what God hath joined, let no man separate."

This article aims to point out that urban industrial society tends to pull apart this natural order and that living on the land is not only the antidote to the problem, but also the ideal to strive for, especially for the Catholic family. It should be stated that a life on the land is not a guarantee of holiness. Certainly not. Neither is city living a guarantee of moral degeneracy. However it is certain that each exerts an opposite influence on the individual and the family – one for the good, and the other towards evil.

The Church Leads the Way

Among modern social critics, there are a few who speak out against such alienation. I will call them agrarian-decentralists. It is no coincidence that many of them are Catholics and those who aren't (or who give no indication that they are) often recognize the Church as taking the leading role in fighting for the true dignity of man. This is of no surprise as only the Catholic Church has preserved an understanding of the true nature of man.

E. F. Schumacher (economist, former head of planning at the British Coal Board, and, oddly enough, a modern-day Distributist) states in his book *Small is Beautiful*:

> Over the last 100 years no one has spoken more insistently and warningly on this subject than have the Roman Pontiffs. What becomes of man if the process of production takes away from work any hint of humanity, making of it a merely mechanical activity? The worker himself is turned into a perversion of a free being.[1]

Schumacher then quotes Pius XI: "And so bodily labor which even after original sin was decreed

[1] E.F. Schumacher, *Small is Beautiful* (New York, NY: Harper & Row, 1973), p. 36.

by Providence for the good of man's body and soul, is in many instances changed into an instrument of perversion; for from the factory dead matter goes out improved, whereas men there are corrupted and degraded."[2]

Again Schumacher states:

> Above anything else there is a need for a proper philosophy of work which understands work not as that which it has indeed become, an inhuman chore as soon as possible to be abolished by automation, but as something decreed by Providence for the good of man's body and soul.[3]

It is no accident that Pius XI's statement draws attention to man's composite nature, i.e., body and soul, because it is here, inside each individual man, that industrial alienation begins to tear apart the natural order. Fr. George Speltz explains these words of Pius XI:

> It is understandable on Thomistic principles why men should suffer degradation through such types of factory labor, and on these same principles the work of the husbandman will be seen to be capable of perfecting man, and compatible with the good life. According to a Thomistic principle of metaphysics and psychology, when man acts, he acts as a person; such is the union of all his component parts and faculties under the rational soul. In all his acts, such as the act of one's hand in labor the person acts; not merely the bodily member. Consequently, the manual labor of a man is more than the repeated physical movements of the members of his body. Manual labor is performed by the person who is endowed with intellect and will. Herein is its dignity. Granted a worthy end, it retains its dignity as long as it involves the functioning of the intellect and the will.[4]

---

[2] *Ibid*, p. 37. [3] *Ibid*, p. 37.

[4] Rev. George Speltz, *The Importance of Rural Life According to*

Rev. Speltz further clarifies by stating:

> Now, the husbandman is in a better position to work as a person than is, for example, the factory worker who must constantly repeat the same simple operation or limited number of operations, and who is in a sense determined *ad unum.* Under this aspect the latter has become dehumanised; and the more complex the machine, the more its operator is determined to one course of action, and the less human is his work.[5]

So if you refer to your work as "mindless," if you sit at a machine doing nothing more than pushing a button or if your work could easily be done by a robot, then your work is degrading you. It is alienating you by continually calling for your will to move your body, but never requiring your mind to do a thing. It is certainly not fulfilling God's desire that your work be for the good of your body and soul.

Neither the Church nor this author is saying that such work is immoral, nor are we saying that such work cannot be meritorious if done with the correct intention and dispositions. What we are saying is that such work is not ideally conducive to the integral well-being of the human person.

Now it may surprise some that the Church has traditionally proposed agriculture to her children as an ideal field of work. And she has done so for many reasons. First, let us consider it as an antidote to the alienation of man within himself, this alienation of man's intellect and will by work. Certainly no one will doubt that agricultural work is physically demanding, but many consider the work of the farmer or stockman to be for the simpleminded. Why else would we have phrases such as "dumb farmer" and

---

the Philosophy of St. Thomas Aquinas (Washington, DC: Catholic University of America Press, 1945), p. 16.

[5] *Ibid*, p. 58.

"stupid hick"? Let us think upon the words of Pius XII who said: "There is indeed no greater mistake than to believe that the tiller of the soil does not need a serious and adequate formation in order to accomplish the varying tasks which mark the seasons in their yearly course."[6]

And again:

> Before the Fall, God had confided to man the cultivation of the earth as the finest and most honourable occupation in the natural order.... To get acquainted with the nature and, so to say, the temperament of his own plot of land, sometimes very different even from that alongside, to find out the germs that are harmful to it, the rodents that burrow in it, the grubs that devour its fruits, the weeds that infest the crops grown therein, to discover in what constituent elements it is deficient, to select the rotation of crops best calculated to enrich it, for these and ever so many other matters, vast and varied information is necessary.[7]

An elderly farmer's wife put the Pope's sentiments in her own words by saying that the good farmer must be a carpenter, a plumber, an electrician, a mechanic, an agronomist, a biologist, and a veterinarian all in one! Thus agriculture requires a tremendous effort of body and mind – a truly human and integrating work.

So far we have treated alienation as it concerns man and himself, but man is not alone in this world or the next, so let us examine alienation through the "lenses" of the hierarchy of being. The hierarchy of being is an ontological categorization of creation and the Creator. In ranked order from greatest

---

[6] Allocution of Pope Pius XII to the Italian Farmers' Federation, November 15,1946, quoted in Rev. Denis Fahey, *The Church and Farming* (Hawthorne, CA: Omni Christian Book Club, 1988), p. 24.

[7] *Ibid*, pp. 24–25.

perfection to least they are God, the angels, man, animals, plants, and mineral matter.

Man has three basic relationships in this hierarchy. The first is his relationship with those above him in the hierarchy, God and the angels. Man has grave obligations in this regard, i.e., to know, love, and serve God in this life. Second, man also relates to other men primarily in the family, but also in the wider community. Third, man has a relation to that which is below him in the hierarchy. Man must be a responsible steward of animals, plants, and mineral matter so that they might serve their immediate purpose – the upkeep of the life – of men and thereby glorify God who established them for this purpose. Man will have to give an account to God in regard to his stewardship of material things.

These are the three basic ways that man relates to creation and his Creator. Industrial work and modern urban society constantly militate against these three basic relations, thus alienating man from his God, his fellow man, and his responsibilities. Despair follows in its wake – a feast of souls for Satan.

The City of God vs. the City of Man

Let us examine, on the other hand, the effect of rural life on each of these relationships. Life on the land speaks directly of God. The husbandman's work consists of releasing a host of natural and organic causes. He is an instrument in the hands of God.

"He taps the font of productivity which God has placed in things. He releases for creative work the mighty potential organic powers of nature, awaiting actualization through him."[8]

[8] Speltz, p. 54.

Pius XII, in a letter to Rev. J.P. Archambault states:

> It cannot be too often repeated how much the work of the land generates physical and moral health, for nothing does more to brace the system than this beneficent contact with nature which proceeds directly from the hand of the Creator. The land is not a betrayer; it is not subject to the fickleness, the false appearances, the artificial and unhealthy attractions of the grasping city. Its stability, its wise and regular course, the enduring majesty of the rhythm of the seasons are so many reflections of the Divine attributes.[9]

William Schaefers, writing on vocations in 1926, makes the obvious comparison. He states:

> The country is the natural habitat of the family and the ideal breeding ground for vocations. For in the country, much more than in the city, the environment is favourable for moulding that character, with its religious hopes and longings, which is desirable in every young man who aspires so high. It can not be denied that there is more peace, more quiet, something more approaching solitude in the country than in the city. And surely peace and quiet are tremendous factors in moulding vocations. Solitude, theologians tell us, stimulates spirituality in man. There is no solitude in the city; there is a turbulence of life there that frequently wearies even the hardened city dweller. The rural spaces preach God more effectively than metropolitan centres. Nature reflects God, and leads to a consideration of its Creator; the cities essentially reflect man, and lead to a consideration of their builders. The city has a way of pounding out the gospel of man; it is continually glorifying the creature; with all the ingenuity possible it caters to the material – the

[9] Letter of Pope Pius XII to Rev. J.P. Archambault, S.J., August 31, 1947; quoted in *The Church and Farming*, p. 5.

> weaker and less important – side of man; it calls to pleasure, fame, and wealth. Life in the country is vastly different. There the soil teaches humility and service, and demands a plodding, working, easily satisfied class of people. In a word, the natural environments in the country are splendid for fostering vocations, while in the city such desirable environments are rarely to be discovered.[10]

This is to say nothing of the blatant immorality which assaults one from every side in the large city. Our cities have now reached such a level of corruption that they are not only spiritually deadly but physically dangerous as well!

The Land and the Family

Rural life has a profound effect on man's relation to others. The basic unit of society is the family, so we shall begin there. There is "...[a] unique relationship which exists between the family and the occupation of agriculture. The farm is the native habitat of the family. Industrial society works against the family and in favour of divorce, desertion, temporary unions, companionate marriage; agricultural society is characterized by the strength, permanence, and unity of the marriage bond and the comparative rarity of its dissolution."[11]

Why is this? Bishop Aloisius Muench explains:

> The family as a social institution is stronger in rural areas than in urban centres. The farmstead is not like a shop, office, or factory to which men and

---

[10] William Schaefers, "Vocations in Rural Districts," *Homiletic and Pastoral Review*, April 1926, pp. 939–940.

[11] National Catholic Rural Life Conference (NCRLC), *Manifesto on Rural Life*, (Milwaukee: Bruce Publishing Company, 1939), pp. 3–4.

> women go in the morning and leave again at night, but it is also a homestead. Where farm ownership is rendered secure the homestead is held in honour by generation after generation as it passes from father to son. The farmstead is for all members an economic unit. Young and old, father, mother, and children have a common stake in it. The vicissitudes of the climate, the approach of the seasons for sowing or harvesting, the land, the seed, the machinery, the fowl and cattle – all evoke a daily interest around the table at meal time or in the evening as the family gathers around the fireside. These are all important elements to hold the family together.[12]

Dr. O.E. Baker further analyses the strength of the rural family by pointing out that in agriculture the family is the economic unit, whereas in industry and commerce the individual is the economic unit.

> In the city, work takes one out of the home, perhaps the wife and mother too must work to support children that, in the city, are economic burdens. In agriculture a wife, or at least a family to live with, is almost essential in operating a farm, and children can work and probably more than pay their way from ten years of age onward.[13]

The wife is meant to be economically productive and in the rural home she does this without ever leaving her family. She often is in charge of the chickens, the milch cow, the garden, the butter, bread, and cheese making, and food preservation. This arrangement is certainly more conducive to holy family living than the working mother spend-

---

[12] Aloisius Muench, "The Catholic Church and Rural Welfare," *Catholic Rural Life Objectives* (Third Series, 1937), p. 6; quoted in *Manifesto.*

[13] O.E. Baker, "The Church and Rural Youth," *Catholic Rural Life Objectives* (Series One, 1935), p. 7; quoted in NCRLC, *op cit.*

ing her hard earned dollars to buy what her country counterpart makes herself.

Baker comments: "In the rural family the aged also have a place – a useful, respected place."[14] This is one of transmitting their knowledge and the fruits of their experience to younger generations. The basics of the art of farming change little over time even though some methods might. Delivering a mal-presented lamb, for example, is not much different today than it was 2,000 or more years ago. This type of work binds the family across generations.

One must not hesitate to make clear that rural life, due to the necessity of having a wife as a helpmate and children to work on the farm, curbs the use of artificial birth control, selfish bachelorism, and lifestyles of unnatural vice of which we are encouraged to be so tolerant. The revered Fr. Vincent McNabb, O.P., leading figure of the English Catholic Back-to-the-Land movement of the 1930's went so far as to argue in *The Church and the Land* that city living, due to the tremendous economic pressure to limit the size of the family, was an occasion of sin and should be fled as any other occasion of sin!

The Land and Society

Not only does man interact with other men in the family, but with other families in the realm of the State. If a State is to be well-ordered, it must consist of well-ordered families made up of well-ordered individuals. It naturally follows that if agricultural labor exerts a positive influence on the individual and the family, then it will be as equally

[14] *Ibid.*

important for the moral and material life of the whole nation. Pope Pius XII said: "We well know how much the moral recovery of the whole people depends on the steadfast faith and social integrity of the tillers of the soil."[15]

Speaking to Italian farmers, Pius XII explained:

> More than others, you live in permanent contact with nature: in material contact, by the fact that your life is passed in places as yet far removed from the excesses of an artificial civilization and is also wholly directed towards producing from the soil, under the beneficent rays of our Heavenly Father's sun, the abundant riches that His loving hand has hidden therein; in contact that is profoundly social also, because your families are not only communities of consumers but, more especially, communities of producers.
>
> From the fact that your life work is so profoundly and at the same time so generally and completely based upon the family, and therefore so fully in conformity with the order of nature, arises the economic strength and, in critical times, the capacity for resistance, with which you are endowed, and also your oft-demonstrated importance in the development of justice and order, public as well as private, throughout the whole people. Finally, the stability of your family life is the reason of the indispensable function you are called upon to exercise as the fount and bulwark of unsullied moral and religious life, as well as the reservoir of men, healthy in mind and body, for all the professions, for the Church and for the State.[16]

The Rev. E. Cahill, S.J., in *The Framework of a Christian State* explains the fundamental impor-

[15] Allocution of Pius XII, *op cit.*
[16] *Ibid.*

tance of the rural family to the well-being of the State. He says:

> Few things are more important for the stability and security of the State than the existence within it of a dominating number of small village and rural proprietors, each enjoying means for a modest but sufficient livelihood, and each secure in the permanent possession of his own small homestead. We have already referred to the well-known social phenomenon that urban families die out after a few generations, and that the urban populations survive only by means of constant supplies from the country. Hence the rural population is the real mainstay of the nation.[17]

It may surprise the reader that the idea of the country as a "reservoir of men" that fed the barren cities was a huge preoccupation of the U.S. hierarchy up to the end of World War II, when they were lulled into a false security by the baby boom. The American Catholic population was overwhelmingly urban and there was a great fear that it would simply die out with the unabated influx of rural Catholics to the cities. Obviously, there are still Catholics in America, but the effects of lower urban birth rates have certainly devastated our ranks.

Cahill continues:

> Besides, as a rule, it is only in the country that the family is attached to a particular locality and a hereditary home. It is this stable rural population whose interests and traditions are intimately associated with the very soil of their country, that form the core and strength of a nation. It is from them that the most vigorous type of citizen comes,

---

[17] E. Cahill, *The Framework of a Christian State* (Fort Collins, CO: Roman Catholic Books. 1997), p. 331.

> and among them that the best fruits of true patriotism are to be found. Hence it has always been the policy of enlightened statesmen to strengthen and stabilize the rural population.[18]

Now if there is one thing lacking today it is enlightened statesmen. Thomas Jefferson, as "enlightened" as he was, still understood the importance of the yeoman in the life of the nation. Such an understanding is beyond the comprehension of our leaders today. They allow our nation, with occasional ineffectual protestations, to slip ever more urban-ward. Actually, they favour policies which exacerbate this problem. Soon we will rely on fewer than 1% of Americans to feed the remaining 99%.

From the point of view of food supply alone this is highly unstable. But if we consider that this is accomplished by the corporatization of agriculture and the destruction of the family farm, then we realize the tremendous loss to the nation of that class which Pius XII calls its "fount and bulwark."

Lest anyone imagine that these teachings of the Church do not apply to the United States for one reason or another, please consider the words of Pius XII in his encyclical letter *Sertum Laetitiae* of November 1, 1939, addressed to the bishops of the United States. The Chief Shepherd first explains that the root of modern social problems is "the refusal to recognize the Divine Majesty" and "the neglect of the moral law." He continues by naming the bitter fruits of such neglect among which is "the flight from the land (*agrorum desertio*)."

One must further lament the destruction of America's agrarian class as its loss is irremediable. Fr. Cahill explains:

> It is comparatively easy to produce an industrial population or a professional class. But a perma-

[18] *Ibid*, pp. 331–332.

nent rural population can not be created to order. Town dwellers can not, as a rule, be successfully transplanted into the country. A peasant population must be the result of a growth of generations.

Hence, Goldsmith's well known words are true:

> "A brave peasantry, the country's pride,
> When once destroyed, can never be
> supplied."[19]

Lastly, we must examine the relation of man to that with which he works. Man is most happy when he works when he can take pride in his work, when he knows that his work is both well done and socially or personally useful. Thus many types of work can be fulfilling. Even the factory worker who mass-produces just one small piece of a much larger whole can take pride in his work, but it would be hard to imagine that it would approach that of a watchmaker carefully making an entire watch from scratch. One must also consider that what is massed-produced is often of poor quality (and this may be totally independent of the intention of individual workers making interchangeable parts) and is often more or less useless or frivolous or downright harmful, morally or otherwise.

Of all of man's work on earth, agriculture is most important because it produces food for the maintenance of the human race and emphasizes man's special relationship with the soil. Bishop Peter W. Bartholome explains:

> Out of the land, the body of man was fashioned, and on it man depends for his continued existence in this world. By the land, man lives and breathes; for its products he expends his life's energy. On the land depends the industry and commerce of the world. The land is basic to all the material activities of man. Through the land man is best able to work

[19] *Ibid,* p. 332; Fr. Cahill quotes *Man and the Soil.*

> up to the fullest development of his nature as created by God. On the land man is closest to God's creation and should therefore with greater facility work out his soul's salvation. And at the end of his life the body of man again returns and becomes identified with the land. Truly there seems to be no relationship of man with material things so intimate as that of man with the earth.[20]

We can easily picture the farmer who loves not only his work, but his animals, his fields, and the very soil under his feet. I know several such men myself. But can we readily imagine the autoworker who loves the spot welder, the steel worker who loves the coke oven, the factory worker who loves the punch press or injection molding machine, the electronics worker who loves the soldering iron, or the data entry technician who loves the keyboard? There may be such individuals, but they are certainly few and far between because, unlike farming, the nature of such work does not instill in the worker a love for his work.

The Way Forward

Leo XIII, in his encyclical on the conditions of the working class, *Rerum Novarum*, clearly lays out the problems afflicting the urban industrial worker. The Pontiff goes to great lengths to clarify the Church's social doctrine, to defend the true interests of the working class against what Pius XI calls in *Quadragesimo Anno*, "the idols of liberalism," and to outline a path towards the solution of the problem. It is of supreme interest that the Pope stakes his highest hopes not on workers, organizations or decreased work hours or increased pay or

[20] Bishop Peter W. Bartholome, Sermon at St. Francis Xavier Cathedral, Green Bay, Wisconsin, October 13, 1946.

better working conditions, but in eliminating the proletarianized working class altogether by converting them to an owning class.

The Pope states: "We have seen, in fact, that the whole question under consideration cannot be settled effectually unless it is assumed and established as a principle, that the right of private property must be regarded as sacred. Wherefore, the law ought to favour this right and so far as it can, see that the largest possible number among the masses of the population own property."[21]

And it is not just any property that the Pope has in mind. He continues:

> But if the productive activity of the multitude can be stimulated by the hope of acquiring some property in land, it will gradually come to pass that, with the difference between extreme wealth and extreme penury removed, one class will become neighbour to the other. Moreover, there will surely be a greater abundance of the things which the earth produces. For when men know that they are working on that which belongs to them, they work with far greater eagerness and diligence. Nay, in a word, they learn to love the land cultivated by their own hands, whence they look not only for food but for some measure of abundance for themselves and their dependents. All can see how much this willing eagerness contributes to an abundance of produce and the wealth of the nation. Hence, in the third place, will flow the benefit that men can easily be kept from leaving the country in which they have been born and bred; for they would not exchange their native country for a foreign land if their native country furnished them sufficient means of living.[22]

Now herein lies not only the solution of the problems of the modern worker, but of the modern

---

[21] Leo XIII, *Rerum Novarum*, §46. [22] *Ibid*, §47.

world's instability as well. For if we could transform the property-less masses into land-owning proprietors then we would resolve what Pius XI terms the "twin rocks of shipwreck."[23]

This same Pope explains in *Quadragesimo Anno*: "There is, therefore, a double danger to be avoided. On the one hand, if the social and public aspect of ownership be denied or minimized, the logical consequence is 'Individualism,' as it is called; on the other hand, the rejection or diminution of its private and individual character necessarily leads to some form of 'Collectivism.'"[24]

Thus we go a long way in preventing "the needy and helpless masses with minds inflamed and always ready for disorder"[25] from taking up the flags of Nazi State Socialism, Communism, and materialistic Capitalism. It is this path, outlined by the Catholic Church, that will, when carried out with "Justice guiding and charity helping"[26] and accompanied by a true return of the nations to Our Lord Jesus Christ, lead us to "a kingdom of truth and life; a kingdom of holiness and of grace; a kingdom of justice, love, and peace."[27]

Can We Get There from Here?

If we are serious Catholics, we will want to take to heart and seriously consider the recommendations of the Church concerning the tremendous benefits of living on the land. If you are a farmer or a rancher, you should meditate on the teachings of the Church. You should strive to take full

---

[23] Pius XI, *Quadragesimo Anno*, §46. [24] *Ibid.*

[25] Leo XIII, *Rerum Novarum*, §66.

[26] Pius XII, *Sertum Laetitiae*, §34.

[27] Preface, Mass of Christ the King.

advantage of your state in life. When you realize the profound dignity of your work, you will have a great supernatural motivation to persevere even though materially things are difficult and often bleak.

If you are a city or suburb dweller, you ought to consider leaving for a more wholesome life on the land. How can it be done? First, let it be known that we ought not reinvent the wheel nor repeat the mistakes of previous generations. Communal settlements and groups of families establishing rural lives together almost always fail. Neither should we go and buy our own farms. Fr. Patrick T. Quinlan explains:

"The average city dweller, no matter what success has been his in other fields, could not become a successful farmer even should he earnestly desire to do so. Farming is a tradition, a way of life, moreover a family way of life, handed down from father to son and from mother to daughter."[28]

Although there are exceptions to this rule, they are so few as to make such an attempt foolish. What then are we to do? The National Catholic Rural Life Conference, established in 1923, vigorously promoted the solution throughout the 1930's and 40's – the rural homestead. The Conference distinguished between a farm and a homestead. Whereas the farmstead is established upon an acreage sufficiently large to support the family through agricultural pursuits, the rural homestead is established upon a small acreage upon which the family dwells and from which the bread winner goes forth to the nearby place of occupation that he might earn the cash income for the family.[29]

The production of such a homestead is primarily to supply as many needs of the family as pos-

---

[28] Rev. Patrick T. Quinlan, *The Rural Homestead* (NCRLC pamphlet).

[29] NCRLC, *Standing on Both Feet* (pamphlet), 1947.

sible. Thus, by nature, it is highly diversified and labor-intensive. There is plenty of work for children. A typical homestead would have a large garden, a few pigs, perhaps a march cow or dairy goats, some sheep, certainly chickens, fruit trees, and whatever else the family found that they could practically and profitably raise for themselves. Often such homesteads would develop one or more sideline businesses such as selling eggs to neighbours or strawberries to passers-by. The twin mottoes of the rural homestead are "Work in the city, live on the land" and "It isn't what you earn that counts, it's what you save." On a practical "how-to" level, the best resource is another experienced homesteader, but since the rural homesteader can be secure with his cash income, he is free to learn by trial and error. There are still today books in print originally published over 50 years ago that are excellent starting points for the aspiring homesteader such as *The Have More Plan, Five Acres and Independence*, and *Ten Acres Enough.*

The rural homestead is practical for any family with a will to do it. One can rely on income from one's city job, move to a small acreage in the country, and slowly build upon the various elements of the homestead. It is a learn-as-you-go situation and one would be free to expand it at his own pace. Most importantly, it enables the family and the individual to reap nearly all of the supernatural benefits pointed out above that result from life on the land. That is in accordance with God's natural order. Of course these benefits would be in proportion to the seriousness of the homestead operation and the will of the family to reap the benefits.

The Better Life

by Willis D. Nutting

Men of heroic character can live a Christian life under any social conditions. Consequently there has been no age so dark as to lack its saints. But there is no doubt that some environments are better than others for the development of sanctity, and that the Church is concerned with bringing about an environmental situation in which unheroic ordinary people are helped rather than hindered in their attempt to live holily. Otherwise an encyclical on the reconstruction of the social order would be beside the point.

In a social order in which injustice abounds and in which many persons are the victims of exploitation, two tasks face the Christian community. The most obvious thing to be done is to take up the cause of the victims of society – to bind up the broken, to curb the power of the oppressor, to live with the down-trodden and to take Christ to them. In this task there is opportunity for the greatest devotion and self-sacrifice, and for the calling forth of the heroic element in man. But this is not the only thing to be done. The Christian community must also take thought in the matter of creating a social order which is more in keeping with the Christian ideal.

Human persons being limited in their abilities, it is to be expected that some Christians will concentrate their attention on one of these tasks, some on the other; and since we most of us see rather narrowly, it is unfortunately true that we are somewhat inclined to disparage the task that does not occupy our interest. Those who throw themselves heroically into the work of caring for the victims of society are frequently impatient with men who withdraw from the sight of distress in order to plan a better environment; and these in turn are likely to question the wisdom of devoting one's life solely to first aid rather than to cures.

Therefore, in discussing the values to be found in rural living and a certain withdrawal from industrial society, I would in no way wish to belittle the great glory of those who identify themselves with that society in order to save its victims. I am simply occupied with another task, one which I believe to be equally important if not as obviously urgent. When a person is responsible for a family, indeed, the urgency is the other way, and the seeking of the best possible living conditions becomes the obvious primary responsibility.

We must make a distinction between rural living and farming, for there is much farming which is almost entirely without those values that we will discuss. A ten-thousand-acre wheat farm, for instance, owned by a corporation whose *members* live in Chicago, run by an expert manager who is there only in season, and having its work done by transient labor – such an institution is merely an outdoor factory and carries with it the evils of the factory system unrelieved by legislation.

We can exclude also the country homes of the wealthy, where life does not differ too much from the Park Avenue apartment except that there are more trees around, and one can play tennis or go riding without the fatigue of a journey away from home.

For our purposes, rural living means life centered in a country home where at least some of the processes traditionally associated with agriculture are carried out. It may be a family farm, or it may be a part-time farm or a "homestead." In any case it will be the center of other activities besides the eating, sleeping, and entertaining which are the chief occupations carried on in the city apartment.

What are the opportunities in this type of living which make it, we believe, the best environment for people to live in? Since the values directly associated with the family are being treated elsewhere, we will deal with the spiritual values offered by rural living in the spheres of work, association, appreciation, and responsibility.

One of the most dismal things about the truly urban man is that he does not understand work, for he has not experienced it. Of course he knows physical exhaustion and mental drudgery; he has nervous breakdowns and high blood pressure, and he dies of coronary thrombosis – but all these things happen to him not because he works but because he does not work. This requires explanation.

For real work to be done several elements must necessarily be present: (1) the mind conceives something to be done; (2) the hand, aided by tools, carries out the conception through the manipulation of certain (3) raw materials. The result is (4) a new creation, either something made, or some change brought about in the physical situation. When a man presides in this whole process – when his mind and hand work together, using his tools and his materials, to produce something which, when it is produced, is his, then he is really working. And this work is one of the greatest things man can do, both in the way of education and of satisfaction, for in it he is realizing a part of his likeness to God. Man is not only *homo sapiens*; he is also *homo faber*, man the maker. It is his nature to work. When he cannot work he is restless and discontented.

In our modern world, with craftsmen almost extinct and artists an infinitessimal and professional minority, the rural home supplies almost the only setting in which a person can work. Elsewhere the planner does not carry out his plans and therefore performs only part of what he is fitted to do. The man who toils does so by carrying out the plans made by someone else, and he also performs only a mutilated function. Neither of them possesses the thing made as a result of the planning and the toil. That belongs to someone who has done nothing but furnish the money. Thus all the people concerned with the production of things are acquainted merely with isolated aspects of the work process. They are not doing what by nature they are designed to do. And as a consequence their labor is a chore, an unpleasant necessity which they indulge in as little as possible. They become abnormally interested in recreation and live for the weekend and the vacation.

There is indeed a kind of parody on work carried out by the men at the top of our economic system. They make plans and carry them out, and have the satisfaction which this brings with it. But such activity is not a coordinated effort of mind and body – these men still have to play golf to keep themselves from obesity – and thus does not have the full value of work. Moreover, it has a great disvalue in the field of morality, for the captains of finance and industry use men as tools and raw materials of their planning; and thus they commit the fundamental immorality of treating human beings as means rather than as ends. This misuse of men carries with it its own punishment, for it brings about in the one who does the misusing a ruthlessness that is the principal ingredient in the corruption which accompanies power.

The opportunity for real, soul-satisfying work, so rare in our day, is found abundantly in rural living. Here a man can make long-range plans and can carry them out without exploiting his fellow men; for the things that he uses are things that exist to be used: soil, plants, animals, building materials, etc. He can live a whole life of work without once using another man as a mere means for carrying out his plans. And neither does he become a tool of someone else. With the materials at hand he can employ the splendid coordination of mind and hand to create something of value for his family. He can fulfill his nature in real work. And this work is much more joyful than any mere recreation. As a matter of fact this work carries with it its own recreation, so that the man who works does not have to worry about how he is going to have his good times. The work itself is a good time even though it be hard. There is a joy in toil which the football player knows not. It is a quiet joy that comes from the knowledge that one has accomplished something, something of real value, and that the accomplishment is his own.

Around me live several men who are "homesteaders." They work in town or in school and live in the country. They spend long hours in the evening working on their land. Their companions on the job or at school go to the movies or play poker in the evenings, but these men work at home. Their companions spend money; they save it. And when you talk with these men you come to realize that their interest, their real life, is in what they do at home. On the job they are carrying out someone else's plans. That is drudgery. But at home they are their own masters. They are exercising that autonomy which is necessary to human dignity. These few hours of autonomy constitute for them their real life. Their rural homes give them their one chance to be human.

Rural living also gives to many people their one opportunity of true association. In our prevailing mode of earning a living men either order others around or are themselves ordered around. They command or obey. It is only in their recreation, where nothing serious is attempted, that they meet as equals and make decisions cooperatively. Elsewhere most of their decisions are made for them by men they never see through channels that they do not understand. They do not have the fruitful and dignity-bringing experience of meeting as equals in voluntary association to make decisions on matters of consequence.

In rural living there is perhaps not so much association as there ought to be, but what there is, is of a kind which is valuable. When men meet together *impromptu* to carry out some task that needs to be done there are no commanders and obeyers. They meet as equals, each can give his suggestion from time to time as the work goes on, and the group decides at each stage what ought to be done, all without any formal leadership. The work is accomplished efficiently without anyone being forced simply to obey or to accept a subordinate position in the eyes of his companions. When neighbors meet together to butcher a pig you have an example of this kind of association. As the process goes on there are a good many things that have to be done simultaneously. You find the men doing these various things not by any prearrangement or blueprint, but as it were spontaneously, each person reacting to what he sees that he can best do from moment to moment. And the pig gets butchered and someone has some valuable meat.

Along with this useful activity there has gone a lot of story-telling, joking, and banter that makes the whole undertaking a recreational as well as a food-producing enterprise. It has been hard work, but it has been fun too. Each man who takes part has maintained his dignity as a human person, but the group has worked together to accomplish something that one man alone could not have done. When a person goes to the country to live he is surprised at the number of necessary tasks that are carried out in just the way which combines toil, planning, cooperation, recreation, and social life with the production of something of material value. Many times people of both sexes and all ages are included in the common enterprise, which then becomes also an educational project. There is a heart-warming, satisfying value in this association which neither the factory nor the cocktail party can approach. It is the kind of activity that produces strong families and strong neighborhood communities.

No society can long endure unless the people who compose it have some conception of responsibility. That is, they must be aware that their actions, good and bad, wise and foolish, have consequences which bring well-being or disaster as the case may be; and they must accept the obligation of performing those actions which bring well-being and avoiding those that lead to disaster. In the very complicated, industrialized, interdependent world in which we live it is not easy to trace the lines of cause and effect. The results of one's actions on one's self and on society are by no means immediately discernible. Rewards and punishments are so slow in catching up that we may escape them altogether, and it will seem that what we do has little significance one way or the other. Since our actions have little visible effect we grow lax in our sense of obligation to do the good and avoid the evil. We cease to worry about effects, we become essentially irresponsible. Our own pleasure then becomes the only measure by which we evaluate what we do. We have only to look around us to see this degenerative process at work.

In rural living the consequences of your actions come home to roost. If you do a foolish thing, you suffer. If you procrastinate, you do without something you would like to have. If you are negligent, a project fails. And there will be no doubt as to where the blame lies. The trail from effect to cause leads right back to the guilty one. When I allow a calf to be out in the cold rain and he dies of white scours and we have no veal for the winter, I cannot put the blame on labor or the Republicans or the communists. The finger points at me. I will not do it again. And when my boy leaves a gate open and a goat gets out and eats up his little apple tree, he cannot blame fate or the government for the loss of the tree. There is no better school than rural life for making people realize that they must watch their actions if they want to avoid loss. It is a harsh school, but one learns in it.

One learns both immediate and long range consequences. When you leave the gate open so that the goat eats the tree, the whole damage is done in a matter of a couple of minutes; but the loss of apples will be felt years from now. If I neglect to put in my alfalfa this spring I will be without hay next year. By my carelessness I lose a year. Most of the processes of agriculture are connected with at least an annual cycle, so that what I do now has its results a year from now, and the results that I want for next year must be planned for now. In such a life one cannot live simply in the present. The past and the future are so intimately bound with the *now* that in all one's planning a sweep of time must be considered. This is quite different from living from pay night to pay night, and far more valuable as an exercise in responsibility. It inculcates the habit of far-seeing, and this is necessary for the citizens of any healthy society.

One of the great values of rural living is the worthy standard of appreciation that tends to accompany it. In urban living the accepted opinion concerning what is desirable and what not is one that works for the demoralization of man. Exposed his whole lifetime to the bombardment of advertising propaganda, and finding little satisfaction in the occupation that earns him his bread and butter, the city man can only with difficulty avoid assuming that the twin goals of life are comfort and entertainment. As a countryman, I am literally astounded at the way these two things loom large in the minds of my city friends – good Catholic friends too. The serious consideration they give to the show and to the eating place, the talking they do about it and the glow of anticipation they reveal when looking forward to how they will spend the evening, and the reminiscing afterward, their pride in the "nice things," meaning push-button appliances and tiled bathrooms – all this makes me wonder which of us is crazy, they or I. And the absorbing interest that is centered on the gladiatorial combats in the football stadium! And the constant flow of alcohol inducing the rising volume of hectic laughter at the cocktail party! The whole business is an indication of a mass of false values leading to a counterfeit joy. And then there is the false value that is more serious – the measure of success by the extent to which one can dominate other men.

There is a glitter to these fake goods that is attractive everywhere. It pulls people to them out of all ways of life, including the rural way. But the rural life seems to be about the only environment in which a person can put up a successful fight against these false values by putting into practice some alternatives. Here, because of so many opportunities of comradeship through common enterprise, one can learn to appreciate the quiet joy of family life, and the association of neighbors. Here one can learn that the joy of creative work far exceeds that pleasure that comes from watching twenty-two men roll in the mud. Here one realizes that the acceptance of responsibility brings a far higher satisfaction than does irresponsible play. Here also necessity requires that accomplishment be rated higher than conspicuous consumption; and a compulsory doing without many things can open the gate to a real understanding of the values in an ascetic way of life.

There is no denying that these values which one can learn to appreciate in rural living are more normal to man and more healthy for society than are those which the urban life encourages, and that therefore the rural home supplies a better environment in this respect than does the home in the city.

From the standpoint of both individual and social well-being, therefore, the idea of reconstructing the social order by bringing people into closer contact with the soil is not the absurdity that our socialistically minded reformers would have us believe. Neither is it so impossible of realization as one might think, but that is another story.

The *forward to the land* movement can take its place as one of the intellectually respectable plans of reform. In itself it is not specifically Christian. It supplies a basis for a healthy natural society upon which a Christian culture can be founded, but it will not of itself supply that culture. It does, however, set forth a kind of association, a way of doing things, and a scale of values which are compatible rather than antagonistic to Christianity. That is more than can be said of urban society.

The Economics of the Catholic Family

by Walter John Marx

Any talk of the economics of the big Catholic family will always come to the problem of providing for additional babies and aged parents. Modern suburbia is often an occasion to sin against duty in these areas. Radical analysis of how to insure a stable and vigorous Catholic population points to a rural environment.

In the early Spring of 1948, a National Conference on Family Life was held in Washington. Depending upon each speaker's particular background and religious and social beliefs, there was much disagreement over the path that should be taken to strengthen the family as the key unit of society. With some exceptions, however, there was general agreement that things were not entirely well with the American family. The rising tide of juvenile delinquency furnished evidence hard to refute on this point. But at the conference, and later, many of the reforms suggested ran counter both to our democratic traditions and to the teachings of the Church regarding the role of the family in society.

Perhaps the most dangerous trend of our times in this respect is to emphasize remedies which, in fact, if not in theory, hasten the disintegration of the family. There appears to be a general distrust of parents by the sociologists, psychologists, and social workers. For example, the United States Commissioner of Education at the end of the school term in 1948 suggested that the long summer vacation be abolished for school children on the theory that it was better to have the children under school supervision than under that of their parents. Organized play and after-school activities, designed to keep idle hands busy, do withdraw the children from an additional segment of family life until the home becomes a combination dormitory and light-lunch establishment. Family activities appear to have little place in the planning of those professional planners concerned with the problems of modern youth.

I have no intention here of repeating once more the general Catholic stand regarding the family. As a one-time professor of history I can say that I know of no civilization that has long endured without a vigorous family life. One of the early marks of the disintegration of a civilization is the decay of family life, a decline in marriages, an increase in divorces and a refusal to have children. Most Catholics give at least lip service to the Catholic ideal of the family, although the decline in the Catholic birth rate, as the Catholic family moves upward in the economic bracket, leads one to suspect that in actual practice, Catholics are often little better than their neighbors.

Without attempting to defend Catholics who give in to the ways of the world, I should like to discuss at some length the economic factors affecting the observance by Catholics of the Church's teaching regarding the family. For the sake of clarity and because of the limitations of space, I may have to oversimplify somewhat the problem and the solution. The reader, however, will have no trouble in filling in the qualifications and the elaborations which should go with the discussion.

We all know the purpose of Christian marriage. The matter is discussed frequently from the pulpit and in the Catholic Press. However, let us take a typical case and see just what happens to a young Catholic couple attempting to carry out the teachings of the Church in a materialistic world ruled largely by the "iron laws" of economics. Before marriage, Joe and Mary had many discussions regarding the economic base of their marriage. Joe, being a young man, was not making a great deal of money. Perhaps Mary had a stenographer's job and it was decided that both would keep on working until the first baby arrived, or until they had an apartment or a small home furnished. Being an average young couple they could not hope to buy their own place.

The first year of marriage was not too difficult. In view of the housing shortage, they were quite happy in finding a one-room efficiency apartment. Their wedding presents and their combined incomes enabled them to furnish their small place rather nicely. Their first real economic problem came with the arrival of the baby. In spite of their combined incomes, they somehow had not been able to save up sufficient money to pay for the hospital and doctor bills. Joe had taken out hospital insurance, but the baby arrived before he could use the insurance for the hospital bill. Then there were the many expenses he had not thought about: a crib, diapers, a sudden surge in the laundry bill, periodic doctor bills for monthly check-ups of the baby, bottles, a sterilizer, etc. Later came prepared baby foods, a baby carriage, clothes, etc. And now the family was forced to live on a single salary. The one-room apartment became impossible. Besides, the landlord gave them an eviction notice because children were not allowed in his apartment house and the baby annoyed the neighbors. Then came the dreary search for a larger apartment in a building tolerating children. Because of the expenses caused by the baby, it was necessary to get a larger place for a rental no higher and preferably lower than the first place. Incredible though it seems, Joe and Mary did find such an apartment, but in a shabbier section of town. They were unable to buy any additional furniture but at least they had a place for the baby's crib.

The cost of the second baby was not so high. Hospital insurance took care of most of the hospital bill, although the hospital authorities found some thirty dollars that was not covered by insurance. Many of the things purchased for the first baby could be used for the second baby. They did have to buy another crib and their daily cost of living mounted as they took care of two babies. They sold the old car Joe had before his marriage and they found it more and more difficult to buy clothes for themselves. Because of the cost of the diaper service, Mary now began to wash her own diapers.

Joe received a modest raise in pay the third year, but this did not equal the rise in the cost of living index and took no account of his increasing family responsibilities. I won't go on and describe the later history of Joe and Mary. Inexorably, each additional baby meant for them a lowering of their standard of living, a further push toward the slum. As the children grew, there were shoes to buy, the food bill went up, clothes became an increasing expense. School proved to be an additional burden.

Worst of all, from the point of view of the parents, their children were being raised in an unhealthy environment of city streets and parking lots, whizzing autos, idle playmates with temptations and false values on all sides. Except for the mysterious workings of God's providence, which somehow enables families such as Joe and Mary's to survive, one does not see why their family should not eventually disintegrate into the hands of the welfare agencies as the economic burden becomes insupportable.

In its advocacy of family allowances, the Church has an answer for part of the problem presented above. However, the most generous family allowance yet voted by any government cannot begin to equal the actual cost of raising a child. The environmental factors mentioned above remain even with a family allowance. A recent survey indicated that of church members in the United States, the Baptists and the Catholics were the poorest. We know that we Catholics are concentrated particularly in the great Eastern cities. Monsignor Ligutti, O.E. Baker, and others have drummed into us over and over again the undeniable fact that our great cities cannot reproduce themselves. This means that the Catholic Church in America, anchored in the big cities, is faced ultimately with a declining membership unless sufficient converts can be made to counteract the declining birth rate of the cities. Because of the factors noted above, we cannot assume that Catholic urban families will reverse the normal urban trend. The history of the Catholics in Quebec who have moved to the cities demonstrates this fact.

What, then, is to be done? Obviously, one of the first things is to attempt to change the environment of the family to one more favorable for family health and well-being. Urbanism ultimately means death for the family. Each additional child means a lowering of the family's standard of living and the necessity of finding larger housing quarters.

Instead of starting off in a city apartment, Mary and Joe could have purchased an acre or two of land in the country within commuting distance of Joe's job. In order to get a home for themselves, they could have lived in even a prefabricated garage and done without modern improvements until they could pay for them out of the money they would otherwise have spent for rent. Perhaps their families, on weekends, could help them build at least a cinder-block or frame shell in which they could live while finishing it off. Or perhaps parish guilds or young men's organizations could, in a weekend or two, throw up a shell much in the spirit of the old house-raisings in colonial America. A garden, a couple of goats or a cow, and perhaps a pig or two and a few chickens would, in the long run, be more profitable to the family than Mary's job in the city, and as the children arrived, the extra food cost would not be so apparent. At a surprisingly early age, the children could begin to share in the responsibility of providing food for the family by taking care of some of the livestock.

In place of the crowded city environment, the children would grow up in the open air with plenty of play space. By choosing the cheaper land, well off a busy highway, money is saved and the children kept from an untimely death from a passing auto or truck. I know one man with a larger place who, with the birth of every son, plants a sufficient number of trees on his place to grow up into marketable lumber by the time his son is ready for college so that his expenses will be paid. With one more child eating eggs, it is no great burden to the family to add a hen or two to the laying flock.

With food and shelter taken care of, most of the battle is won. A home-built house can easily be expanded to take care of new little residents. In my own case, for example, now that our fifth baby has arrived, I am preparing to change the shed roof of part of our structure to a gable roof giving me space for a room upstairs. My oldest boy, five at the end of October, is the owner of a seven-month old milk goat and is already being trained in its care and management. Little Lois, a year younger, helps us feed the chickens every day and even little Anton who is just three, helps his mother bring in the laundry from the line.

When youngsters reach their teens in the city, they are still heavy and, indeed, increasing burdens upon their families. In the country, by that time, they are already more than paying their own way through the aid given in developing the various home enterprises. Their work teaches them self-reliance, responsibility and resourcefulness. They learn there is no magical way to get the things they need and want without working for them.

I am restricting myself to a discussion of the economic basis of the family, but the reader will easily realize that there are even more important considerations involved in the sort of family I am describing, the additional strength of a family in which each member takes some part in the family enterprise, the family planning involved in which the children are encouraged to take a part, the health that comes from outdoor living and exercise, the constant evidence of God's work when one labors with growing things, the skills that are acquired easily and naturally. Every one of my boys, by the time he is seventeen, will have a rough mastery of the carpenter's, mason's, plumber's and electrician's trades, in addition to the ability to grow things in the soil. He will be able to build his own home with his own hands and in the precarious times ahead will have the versatile background necessary for survival. My girls will have similar training along lines complementing the activities of the boys.

In discussing the economics of the Christian family, I have emphasized the problem of providing for additional babies. But the older folks, too, form part of a family, and one of the many tragedies of our times is the inability of the average family to take over the support of aged parents who, at times, have impoverished themselves in order to give the children a "good start." The city apartment obviously was not designed for the care of one's parents or in-laws. Even if a large enough apartment could be found and paid for, the nervous tension of so many people living so closely together is often too great. Here again, the rural home provides a solution. Additional quarters with extra privacy can be erected at nominal cost. The old man who always seems in the way in an apartment, becomes largely self-sustaining with a garden and a few chickens of his own. He becomes the playmate and the arbiter of his grandchildren. He has new self-respect as he feels that he is pulling his own weight in the family's economy.

For the reasons noted above, an increasing number of families, Catholic and non-Catholic, are deserting the cities for rural environments even when it is necessary in most cases to retain a city job. Few families regret the move although it is absolutely necessary that both husband and wife agree upon the wisdom of making the change before taking the final step. It is helpful also if two or more families with similar ideas settle near enough to each other to permit the women to visit and compare notes. The isolated family can succeed only in the event the woman is remarkably self-sufficient and does not mind the loneliness of a rather secluded life. It is not my purpose in this article to discuss the spiritual and moral development that would be possible in a whole community of such families with its own school and church.

I do not wish to minimize the importance of the family allowance plan. In our present society some such plan is essential, but the money would render more effective help to the large family if the family were in a rural environment where the subsidiary members of the family could produce real wealth at home. The production by the family of as many of its own needs as possible seems to be the only way in which a young couple can bear and rear children in a healthy environment, frugal no doubt, without many modern conveniences, but receiving the essentials of adequate and healthy shelter and good food.

I speak from personal experience. I have heard so many city youngsters plead for the glass of milk their mother did not have, or for the second helping at the table that could not be given. No matter how desperate our situation, so long as we have our land and our cow, my tiny tots have all the rich raw milk they can drink, with none of the vitamins pasteurized out. When the cow goes dry next summer, we expect our two milk goats to come into production. In the meantime, our cow provides also our butter and milk for the neighbor's children until their own goats come in fresh. My children are outdoors from dawn until dark. They have excellent appetites and go to sleep promptly in the evening after their prayers. Before we moved to the country, they were pale and anemic, dawdled over their food and refused to go to sleep without repeated spankings. They copy my efforts in the garden with dime tools I bought for them. They attempt to help me in my building operations and next year I shall buy the oldest some simple carpenter tools. They pick wild berries in season, watch the chickens or play with the goats and the cats. In the evening they will be waiting to meet me, perhaps part way down the gravel road to my place so that they can ride a short distance with me, all talking at once, reciting the day's events and trying to enlist my help in any number of their private enterprises. We have our winter's potatoes from our garden, a laying flock of chickens that supplies us with fresh eggs, and enough of a surplus to pay for the feed and we have made a start at least on growing our own feed. The size of our family means that there are always hand-me-down clothes for the younger ones to wear. Surplus bunk beds from the army solve the sleeping problem. Next year I shall plant a little more food to take care of little Erie who arrived last summer. Attractively-printed feed sacks make clothes for the younger children. I have not yet licked the shoe problem, a very real one with baby shoes at five dollars a pair, but if things got desperate, I would insist on reverting to my boyhood in northern Alaska and make Eskimo-type footgear out of the skins of our own animals.

There are so many advantages to this way of living that I find it difficult to restrict myself to a discussion solely of its economics. There are so many intangible psychological factors involved, the element of stability, the feeling of security which children have when living in a house of their own, surrounded by land that they can never get in a city apartment. Most Europeans look upon America as a matriarchal society since the man seems to exist merely to bring home a salary check. What training the children get outside of school comes primarily from the mother. In the above plan of living, in the evening and on weekends the father is in intimate contact with his children and can assume some of the responsibility for their training. They help in simple tasks, run errands, get a tool I lack for a particular job, and so forth. Even in heavy tasks where my full strength just barely succeeds in balancing some heavy object, the extra push of my two small boys creates the necessary margin for success. Nicky watches me milk the cow every evening and when his hands are a little larger, that is a chore he will take over. There is also a wonderful feeling about being one's own master in the country. My children can make as much noise as they wish. If I want to keep a pig or two, I need ask no man's consent. I have my own water supply. I could get my own fuel from my woods. There are fish, crabs and oysters just off my property and the only reason I have not enjoyed them so far is that I have spent my spare time in building and cultivating. In two or three years the boys will enjoy fishing and crabbing and will be able to satisfy their mother's love of sea food.

As I have mentioned above, God's providence is the only explanation we can give for the success of so many large families raised under incredible difficulties in urban slums. But we should take advantage of the natural means God has given us in order to make easier the raising of a Christian family. We can increase in sanctity by resisting our daily temptations. At the same time we are taught not to expose ourselves willfully to occasions of sin. For many people the city is just such an occasion of sin. The economic pressure alone leads to birth control, if not to outright thievery and embezzlement. The problem is critical for the Church in America and it will be necessary to multiply the efforts of the National Catholic Rural Life Conference many times if we are to insure a stable and vigorous Catholic population in the next century, or, dare I say, in the next depression when the abject dependence of the urban population will at once become apparent.

Two Articles on Distributism:
An Introductory Note

When considering the topics raised by the following two articles, "Distributism: Economics as if People Mattered," and "Why and How for a Parallel Economy," there will be a tendency, engendered by the mind-numbing din of the Liberal Establishment media, to view the macro-economic discussion of Distributism as something of mere historical interest and the micro-economic proposals for implementing the Distributist idea as simply idealistic and "imprudent." And, yet, when we consider the economic and social consequences of Capitalism, as these were encountered by the Corporatists and Distributists of the 19th and 20th centuries, we cannot help but shake our heads with amazement at the obvious fact that the problems which they saw as necessitating a change of course from policies of economic liberalism have grown exponentially in our own day. Moreover, the politicians, the behind-the-scenes shapers of mass public opinion, and, subsequently, the English-speaking populace at large of the 1920s and 30s were no more amenable to the answers to the problem of economic liberalism given by Chesterton, Belloc, Penty, and the German and French corporatist thinkers, than are those same groups in our own day. When considering these articles' real attempt to contribute to the revival of the Distributist idea as a serious macro-economic goal and ideal for rational men's minds, along with the presentation of realizable beginnings for a Distributist plan for local traditional communities, we must ask ourselves whether there are fewer mass bankruptcies of individuals, corporations, and nations than there were in the 1920s and 30s, whether the average man has become less dependent on the usurious credit system than was his grandfather, and whether the possibility of unemployment and catastrophic indebtedness has become less of a worry for the working man than it was 60 years ago? For those who will think through these questions with an honest mind, the answer is clearly NO!

The task that confronts the serious thinker and doer who is attracted to the economic "Third Way" is to gain an understanding of the history and doctrinal and ideological roots of the Distributist/Corporatist movement. We must grasp again the fact that this was the response of serious Catholic thinkers to the challenge posed by Liberal Capitalism and Socialism to the proper order of human society as that order had been lived in the ages of the Christian past. The times, however, require not only serious thought and prayer, but *also* serious social action. The proposals made in the article "How and Why for a Parallel Economy" can all be implemented practically and legally in the nations of the English-speaking world. The only thing that is necessary is that men of conviction will this type of community building. The construction of a "parallel economy" on the local level will be one of the most efficacious ways of "disinvesting" in a godless and exploitative System and investing in new homesteads of Christendom.

Dr. Peter E. Chojnowski

Distributism: Economics as if People Mattered

by Dr. Peter E. Chojnowski

In truly "prophetic" utterances, the analysis of present circumstances, along with a consideration of the laws written into human nature which manifest themselves in history, can yield a prediction concerning the general outline of things to come. This judgement of the well-informed and perceptive mind is somewhat undermined by only one factor. The universe, and the "universe" of human society in which the inherent laws written into human nature by its Creator reveal themselves in historical events, is also a universe which contains free creatures who are undetermined as regards the means they can employ to achieve their specifically human end. Human freedom inserts a variable in the material necessity of the universe. This contingency and variability has its ultimate source in the spirituality of the human soul. It is precisely on account of his materialistic rejection of the human soul that Karl Marx, for instance, could make such ridiculously precise predictions as to the "necessary" movement of economic, political, and social history. This does not mean, however, that there is not an inherent natural law which determines which human endeavours will "work" and which will lead to catastrophe. During the 19th and early 20th centuries, there were a group of scholars, theologians, philosophers, social critics, and poets, who predicted the inevitable demise of the capitalist economic system which was just developing in Continental Europe, but had been operative for 100 years in England. When you read their works, especially the English authors of the early 20th century – here we include Hilaire Belloc, G.K. Chesterton, and Arthur Penty – one is struck by the fact that their analyses are more valid today than they were 70 or 80 years ago, their predictions more likely to be imminently fulfilled. What they predicted was nothing less than the collapse of the capitalist system. In the case of Belloc, in his book *The Servile State*, it was predicted that Capitalism would soon transform itself into an economic and social system which resembled the slave economies of the pre-Christian and early Christian eras.

Why did they predict such a collapse or inevitable transformation? In their writings, many reasons are given; however, we can narrow them down to three. The first they referred to as the "capitalist paradox." The paradox is a consequence of Capitalism being an economic system which, in the long run, "prevents people from obtaining the wealth produced and prevents the owner of the wealth from finding a market." Since the capitalist strives both for ever greater levels of production and lower wages, eventually "the labourer who actually produces say, boots cannot afford to buy a sufficient amount of the boots which he himself has made." This leads to the "absurd position of men making more goods than they need, and yet having less of those goods available for themselves than they need."[1]

---

1 Hilaire Belloc, *Economics for Helen* (Hampshire, England: St. George Educational Trust, n.d.), p. 62.

The second reason is now more pertinent than when it was first given. The capitalist system, by its very nature, places the preponderance of wealth in the hands of a small minority. This monopoly on the money supply by banking and financial concerns becomes more absolute as the capital-needing consumer must go to the banks to borrow money. Usury, now called "interest," insures that those who first possess the money for loan will end up with a greater portion of the money supply than they possessed before the loan was issued. As wages stagnate and interest payments become increasingly impossible to make, massive numbers of defaults will inevitably produce a crisis for the entire financial system.[2] When entire nations default on loans, there will be a crisis throughout the entire international financial system. Demise is, therefore, built into the very structure of the capitalistic system in which capital (i.e., all kinds of wealth whatsoever which man uses with the object of producing further wealth, and without which the further wealth could not be produced. It is a reserve without which the process of production is impossible)[3] is primarily in the hands of the few. As G.K. Chesterton rightly stated, the problem with Capitalism is that it produces too few capitalists!

The third fact concerning Capitalism, which the Distributists thought would inevitably bring down the system or lead to its fundamental transformation, was the general instability and personal insecurity which marks a full-blown capitalist economy. What accounts for this general feeling of insecurity and instability, which characterizes both the individual "wage-earner" and the society living under

---

[2] Cf. Hilaire Belloc, *Usury* (Hampshire, England: Saint George Educational Trust, n.d.).
[3] Belloc, *Economics*, p. 13.

Capitalism, is both the always-present fear of unemployment and, hence, of destitution, and the fact that a laborer's real wages leave him with only enough money to cover the expenses of the day. Saving, so as to provide an economic hedge against the misfortune of unemployment or personal crisis, becomes almost impossible.[4]

The above were only some of the reasons why the Distributists, who formed the *Distributist League* in 1926, thought that the capitalist economy would eventually collapse. These were not, however, the only problems which they found with the system.

The social consequences of the majority being unable to afford real property, the decline and eventual disappearance of the trade guilds and vocational corporations, the "necessity" of wives and mothers entering the "work force," the end of small-scale, family-owned businesses and farms, and the decline of the apprentice system were all indictments of Capitalism in the minds of those who sought to chart out a "third way" beyond Capitalism – which is simply liberalism in the economic sphere – and Socialism.

There is little doubt that the problems with Capitalism, which were cited by the Distributists, have only grown in their proportion in our own time. The concentration of wealth, exemplified by the recent merger of Citicorp and Travellers – which produced the largest banking institution in the United States with assets of $700 billion, simply boggles the mind. The institution of usury, always a necessary adjunct of economic liberalism, has caused in recent years more bankruptcies and personal debt than ever before in history. Nations such as Indonesia are tottering on the brink of

[4] Arthur Penty, *The Guild Alternative* (Hampshire, England: The Saint George Educational Trust, n.d.), p. vi.

social, economic, and political chaos because of their inability to pay the interest on their hundreds of billions of dollars in bank debt. If such a nation should go into default, it could threaten to throw a whole variety of nations into recession, depression, or worse.

It is not proper to say that the predictions of the imminent demise of Capitalism were totally without fulfilment. The 1920's, 30's, and 40's witnessed reaction after reaction to the radical individualism which is the fundamental idea of liberal capitalism. Truly, the market is the institutionalization of individualism and non-responsibility. Neither buyer nor seller is responsible for anything but himself.[5] The idea that if every man simply seeks after his own economic interest, all will be provided for and prosper, was almost universally rejected during these decades. We see strong reactions to economic liberalism in Russian Communism, German National Socialism, Italian Fascism, Austrian, Portuguese, and Spanish Corporatism, British Fabian Socialism, along with American "New Deal" leftism. Thus, in the 1930s and 1940s, most of the world was ordered by ideologies which explicitly rejected the premises of economic liberalism. We must also not forget the international economic crash of the late 20s and early 30s, which produced economic depression, totalitarian regimes, and, finally, world war.

There is one fact which separates our day from the days of the 30s and 40s, however. The concentration of wealth and capital, the inadequacy of a man's pay to provide the basics of life and to provide for savings for the future, the lack of real

---

[5] E.F. Schumacher, *Small is Beautiful: Economics as if People Mattered* (New York: Harper Colophon Books, 1975), p. 42.

property generously and broadly distributed, is masked by the reality of easy credit. Easy credit, which is not ultimately "easy" at all on the borrower, anaesthetizes the populace to the grim facts of capitalist monopoly. Since we seem to be able to get all the things that we want, the reality of real money being increasingly unavailable to the average man is lost in the delusionary state of the consumerist utopia. Only when the "benefit" of usurious credit is cut off do we realize the full extent of the problem. The greatest problem with liberal capitalism, however, is not the concentration of wealth or real property; the greatest "existential" problem created by Capitalism is the problem of the very meaning and reality of work. To work is essential to what it means to be a human being. Next to the family, it is work and the relationships established by work that are the true foundations of society.[6] In modern Capitalism, however, it is *productivity and profit* which are the basic aims, not the providing of *satisfying work.* Moreover, since "labor-saving" devices are the proudest accomplishments of industrial capitalism, labor itself is stamped with the mark of undesirability. *But what is undesirable cannot confer dignity.*[7]

It is not merely that industrial capitalism has produced forms of work, both manual and white-collared, which are "utterly uninteresting and meaningless. Mechanical, artificial, divorced from nature, utilizing only the smallest part of man's potential capacities, [sentencing] the great majority of workers to spending their working lives in a way which contains no worthy challenge, no stimulus

---

[6] *Ibid*, p. 34.

[7] E.F. Schumacher, *Good Work* (New York: Harper and Row, 1979), pp. 27–28.

to self-perfection, no chance of development, no element of Beauty, Truth, Goodness."[8] Rather, Capitalism has so fundamentally alienated man from his own work, that he no longer considers it his own. It is those with the financial monopoly who determine what forms of work are to exist and which are "valuable" (i.e., *useful* for rendering profits to the owners of money).[9] Since man spends most of his days working, his entire existence becomes hollowed out, serving a purpose which is not of his own choosing nor in accord with his final end. In regard to the entire question of a "final end," if we are to consider Capitalism from a truly philosophical perspective, we must ask of it the most philosophical of questions, *why*? What is the purpose for which all else is sacrificed, what is the purpose of continuous growth? Is it growth for growth's sake? With Capitalism, there is no "saturation point," no condition in which the masters of the system say that the continuous growth of corporate profits and the development of technological devices has ceased to serve the ultimate, or even the proximate, ends of mankind. Perhaps, the most damning indictment of economic liberalism, indeed, of any form of liberalism, is its inability to answer the question "why."

A) Corporatism: The Catholic Response

1) The History of the "Third Way"

To understand the history of the "Third Way," a name given to an economic system which is neither Marxist nor Capitalist by French corporatist

[8] *Ibid*, p. 27.

[9] *Ibid*, pp. 27–28.

thinker Auguste Murat (1944), we must consider the social, political, and economic realities which originally motivated its main advocates. Originally, "Corporatism," later to be termed "Distributism" by its English advocates, Hilaire Belloc and G.K. Chesterton, was a response on the part of German traditionalists and Catholics to the inroads which the ideology of the French Revolution had made into their country in the early and middle years of the 19th century. The institutions which were being defended in Corporatist thought were the ancient "estates" or "guilds" which had been the pillars of Christian Germany for centuries. These corporate bodies, grouping together all the men of a particular occupation or social function, were an institutional opposition to the revolutionary doctrines of individualism and human equality. One early rightist thinker, Adam Muller, upheld the traditional idea of social stratification based upon an organic hierarchy of estates or guilds (*Berufstandische*). Such a system was necessary on account of the essential dissimilarity of men. Moreover, such a system would prevent the "atomisation" of society so much desired by the revolutionaries who wished to remake in a new form that which had been pulverized by liberalism.[10]

2) Von Ketteler and the Guild System

It was, however, a German nobleman and prelate, Wilhelm Emmanuel, Baron von Ketteler (1811–1877), Bishop of Mainz, who directed Corporatism into new avenues and forced it to

---

[10] Ralph H. Bowen, *German Theories of the Corporative State* (New York: McGraw-Hill, 1947), p. 18.

address new concerns. The realities which Bishop von Ketteler knew the Catholic mind had to address were industrialism and economic liberalism. As Pope Leo XIII himself admitted on several occasions, it was the thought of Bishop von Ketteler which helped shape his own encyclical letter on Catholic economic teaching, *Rerum Novarum* (1891).[11] The "new things" His Holiness was addressing were Capitalism and Socialism. Both meet with his condemnation, although Capitalism is condemned with strong language as an abuse of property, a deprivation of the many by the few, while Socialism is dismissed outright as being contrary to man's inherent right to own property.[12]

Von Ketteler also, in his book *Die Arbeiterfrage und das Christenthum* (*Christianity and the Labor Problem*), attacks the supremacy of capital and the reign of economic liberalism as the two main roots of the evils of modern society. Both represented the growing ascendancy of individualism and materialism, twin forces that were operating to "bring about the dissolution of all that unites men organically, spiritually, intellectually, morally, and socially." Economic liberalism was nothing but an application of materialism to society. "The working class are to be reduced to atoms and then mechanically reassembled. This is the fundamental generative principle of modern political economy."[13] What Ketteler sought to remedy was "this pulverization method, this

---

[11] *Ibid*, pp. 19 and 79.

[12] Michael Oakeshott, *The Social and Political Doctrines of Contemporary Europe* (New York: The Macmillan Company, 1944), p. 66. Cf. *A History of Distributism*, adopted from an address to the Third Way International Conference, London, October 16, 1994, by Anthony Cooney, editor of the *Liverpool Newsletter*.

[13] Bowen, *op cit*, pp. 80–81.

chemical solution of humanity into individuals, into grains of dust equal in value, into particles which a puff of wind may scatter in all directions."[14] Bishop von Ketteler's solution to this problem of the pulverization of the work force and the ensuing injustice which this would inevitably breed, was to propose an idea which was the central concept of medieval and post-medieval economic life: the Guild system. When responding to a letter from a group of Catholic workers who had submitted the question, "Can a Catholic Workingman be a member of the Socialist Worker's Party?" Bishop von Ketteler outlined the basic structure of these vocational guilds or *Berufstandische*: First, "the desired organizations must be of natural growth; that is, *they must grow out of the nature of things, out of the character of the people and its faith*, as did the guilds of the Middle Ages." Second, "they must have an economic purpose and must not be subservient to the intrigues and idle dreams of politicians nor to the fanaticism of the enemies of religion." Third, "they must have a moral basis, that is, a consciousness of corporative honour, corporative responsibility, etc." Fourth, "they must include *all the individuals of the same vocational estates*." Fifth, "*Self-government* and *control* must be combined in due proportion."

The guilds which von Ketteler was advocating were to be true social corporations, true vocational "bodies" which were to have a primarily economic end, and yet be animated by the "soul" of a common faith. These "bodies," just like all organic entities, would be made up of distinct parts all exercising a unique role in their particular trade. In the days of corporate giants and trade unions, it is, perhaps, impossible to imagine vocational organizations

[14] *Ibid*, pp. 53–57.

which include *both* owners and workers, along with technicians of all types. These organizations would regulate all aspects of their particular trade, including wages, prices for products, quality control, along with certifying that all apprentices have the requisite skills to perform adequately the guild's particular art.

3) The Guild System and Social Solidarity

What these traditional vocational groups were able to foster during the ages in which they ordered the life of the craftsman was a decentralization both of property and of economic power. They also enabled the average craftsman to have a real say in the workings of his trade. Such economic "federalism" or decentralization prevented the development of financial monopolies. As Hilaire Belloc states, "Above all, most jealously did the Guild safeguard the division of property, so that there should be formed within its ranks no proletariat upon the one side, and no monopolizing capitalist upon the other."[15]

B) Chesterbelloc and Distributism

It was in the early years of this century that Hilaire Belloc and G.K. Chesterton, joined by a former Socialist, Arthur Penty, inspired by *Rerum Novarum*, attempted to articulate an economic system which stood on a totally different set of principles than did the "new things" of Capitalism

[15] Hilaire Belloc, *The Servile State* (Indianapolis, Indiana: Liberty Classics, 1977), pp. 78–79.

and Socialism. The name they gave to this system, Distributism, awkward as they themselves realized, expressed not the socialist idea of the confiscation of all private property, but rather, *the wide-spread distribution of land, real property, the means of production, and of financial capital, amongst the greater part of the families of a nation.* Such a concept, along with their encouragement of the Guild system and of a return to the agrarian life, and their condemnation of the taking of interest on non-productive loans, formed the core of this "new" economic model.

In his book, *Economics for Helen,* Belloc identifies the nature of the Distributist State by distinguishing this type of State and social and economic system from that of the Servile State and the Capitalist State. The Servile State is the one of classical antiquity, in which vast masses of the people work as slaves for the small class of owners. In this way, the economic state of antiquity is very similar to the economic system of our own time, insofar as a very small minority possess real property, land, the means of production, and financial capital, while the great mass of the population does not possess these goods to any significant degree. How does Belloc distinguish the Servile State from that of the Capitalist State, in which he counts the Britain of his own time? The difference is that whereas the Servile State is based on coercion to force the greater part of the population, which does not possess property, to work for those who do, the Capitalist State employs "free" laborers who can choose to sign a work contract with one employer or another. In the liberal Capitalist State, one is "free" to choose to apply for work or accept work from one of the various owners of the means of production. In return for this work, the laborer receives a wage which is a small portion of the wealth that he produces.[16]

What distinguishes the Distributist State from the two States mentioned above is that, instead of a small minority of men owning the means of production, there is a wide distribution of property. In this regard, Belloc defines property as "the control of wealth by someone."[17] Property *must*, then, be controlled by someone, since wealth which is not kept or used up by someone would perish and cease to be wealth.

1) England's Journey from Distributism to Capitalism

It is Belloc's historical thesis that it was not the Industrialism of the late 18th and early 19th centuries which brought about the rise of Capitalism, but rather that England was a capitalist state in the making long before the emergence of the railroad or the factory. The Servile State, the state in which a small number of owners controlled the land and the men who worked the land, was a mark of the Roman civilization which gradually transformed itself, under the influence of the Catholic Church, into the feudal system in which the serfs went from being "slaves" who owned nothing, to being "serfs" who could retain (some of) what they produced in the fields. The serf had the right to pass the land down to his own kin and he could not be thrown off his land. Thus, the personal security and economic and social stability which characterized the Roman estate system was carried over into medieval times.[18]

---

[16] *Ibid*, p. 59.
[17] Belloc, *Economics for Helen*, p. 50.
[18] Cf. Belloc, *The Servile State*.

This historical movement, under the aegis of the Church, towards a man working on the land which he himself owned and working for his own benefit and for that of his family, came to an end in England in the 16th century during the reign of King Henry VIII. Since the Distributist State had grown up under the eye of Holy Mother Church, it should not be surprising that it would end when She was attacked and suppressed. According to Belloc, it was King Henry's confiscation of the monastery lands in England, and his action of parcelling them out among his wealthy supporters, which marked the beginning of the transformation of England from a nation in which property, the land, and the means of production were widely distributed, to one in which a small number of families control increasingly greater shares of the land. The coming of Protestantism marked the transformation of the average Englishman from independent yeoman to tenant farmer. The concentration of wealth would occur, then, long before England would become the industrial power of the world in the 19th century.[19]

2) Small is Beautiful

There can be no doubt as to the most general form of family ownership foreseen and advocated by Belloc and Chesterton. For them, the most humane and stable economic system was one in which a majority of families farmed land which they themselves owned, doing it with tools which were also their own.[20] Here they were following the lead of Pope Leo XIII, who in *Rerum Novarum* advocates a similar aim:

---

[19] *Ibid.*
[20] Belloc, *Economics for Helen*, p. 62.

> We have seen therefore that this great labor question cannot be solved save by assuming as a principle that private ownership must be held sacred and inviolable. The law, therefore, should favour ownership and its policy should be to induce as many as possible of the people to become owners.... If working people can be encouraged to look forward to obtaining a share in the land, the gulf between vast wealth and sheer poverty will be bridged.... A further consequence will be the greater abundance of the fruits of the earth. Men always work harder and more readily when they work on that which belongs to them.... And...men would cling to the country of their birth, for no one would exchange his country for a foreign land if his own afforded him the means of living a decent and happy life.[21]

Being Englishmen, the idea that the land meant wealth was inevitably ingrained in their conception of economics. Ownership of the land by the families who themselves worked the land would also mean financial stability, no fear of unemployment, a family enterprise which could engage, in some measure, all members, an ability to put aside food and supplies to create a hedge against destitution, a way of providing not only for one's children but for one's children's children, along with creating an economic structure which is not oriented towards corporate profits but towards providing for familial subsistence and a local market. Belloc speaks of this type of Distributist economy as the one most general throughout the history of mankind, with the possible exception of the slave economy. Capitalism and Socialism are certainly recent interlopers on the human economic scene.[22]

---

[21] Pope Leo XIII, *Rerum Novarum*, §35.
[22] Belloc, *Economics for Helen*, p. 64.

Next we must address the ways in which such a Distributist idea can be implemented on the personal and community level. In this regard, our next article will focus on the concept of a "parallel economy" formed by those who wish to begin to implement the economic teachings of *Rerum Novarum* and *Quadragesimo Anno*, along with focusing on the agrarian idea both as Catholic thought and human good sense.

Why and How for a Parallel Economy

by Dr. Peter E. Chojnowski

When considering the practical implications of the economic doctrines of Distributism, it is important to remember that the theorists Hilaire Belloc, G.K. Chesterton, Arthur Penty, and Fr. Vincent McNabb had no intention of merely providing a macro-economic model for a nation. Such a macro-economic model is useful for the prudential decisions of the statesman. They, more so than we, had hoped that such a model would be taken up by the statesmen of their day. It is providential, therefore, that they also mentioned the micro-economic implications of the "Third Way." It is these micro-economic implications, applied specifically to the current situation of the average traditional Catholic family, which will be the topic of this article.

It is particularly fitting that we focus on the micro-economic aspects of the Third Way and ask ourselves how we can apply these principles and ideas to our own lives, our own family situations, and the situations of our ever-growing traditional Catholic communities. The reason it is fitting is because "economics" from the Greek *oeconomia*, means "household management," the way in which we give order, sustenance, and stability to our families and our communities. A true economic theory must, therefore, have as its primary aims the establishment of a system which provides for the basic needs of families and which provides men with work which is intrinsically fulfilling, capable of providing sustenance, and in full accord with the ultimate end of human life, the sharing in the Divine Life Itself.

What will enable our families to achieve these ends of work and household? First, we must commit ourselves to the goal advanced by the economic teachings of Pope Leo XIII (*Rerum Novarum*), Pope Pius XI (*Quadragesimo Anno*), and the Distributist theorists: the attainment of real property for families. It is only with the attainment of real property (i.e., not mortgaged to the modern day usurer) that we shall establish fixed "realms," footholds of Christendom capable of sustaining, over an indefinite period of time, families dedicated to the Social Kingship of Our Lord Jesus Christ.

Second, we must organize labor. Obviously, to organize labor there must be a sufficiently large "labor pool" to organize. If we are truly to construct the essentials of a micro-economic system, we must fulfil the end of an economic system, the satisfaction of the basic needs of families. This can only be done if there is a diverse enough group of men and women whose occupational talent would allow them to participate in this attempt to provide for the basic and primary needs of a community. In this regard, let us emphasize that our "parallel economy" (i.e., an economy which provides for the same needs as the dominant capitalist economy, but provides for these needs in a different manner) must be focused on attempting to provide what Fr. Vincent McNabb refers to as "primary goods" (e.g., housing, food, clothing, and I would add medical services), as opposed to "secondary goods."

Secondary goods are those which are meant to satisfy some want or whim of man, but are not essential as are primary goods. By providing for the basic needs, or at least as many as possible, our community would advance towards the self-sufficiency which is the mark of all true societies.

Third, we need to have, on the part of a coherent community organized on the foundation of the true Faith, a commitment to support, in every way possible, the economic organization of the community on the basis of the teachings of the Church. Without this type of intentional commitment, any such project will fail. What is needed is both an occupational commitment on the part of some members of the community or communities, and a financial commitment on the part of all of the members of a community. What type of occupational commitment would this entail? It would mean that a workingman or professional would give up his capitalistic consciousness which dictates that he use his skills, talents, and labors to fulfil the wants and whims of himself and his family alone, but rather use them to both satisfy his families needs and contribute to the satisfaction of the needs of all the families in the community. What type of financial commitment would this entail? Only the resolve, on the part of all the members of the community, to channel their financial resources in such a way that their own family's needs are satisfied through the efforts of the economic organs or corporate bodies which are made up of the men and women of one's own community. The point is not gratuitous financial contributions, but rather simply fulfilling one's family's basic needs within the structures organized by the community itself. For this especially to occur, we must develop a stronger sense of "brotherhood" based upon adherence to the fullness of the true Faith and upon the God-given virtue of fraternal charity. Our commitment, as individuals and as communities, must be to ensure that whole groups of families, the larger the better, survive, prosper, raise and educate their children, and persist in their practice of the true Religion in the face of a completely hostile world and anti-Christian "system." This would be our opportunity to disinvest in an economic system committed to the destruction of large, truly Catholic families and reinvest in a micro-economic effort that will not only sustain traditional Catholic families as traditional Catholic families, but, inevitably, help sustain the traditional chapels and schools which are now giving life to the souls and minds of so many.

A) Guilds

The first step in the organization of such a micro-economic system is the organization of guilds. Guilds were the organs of the Distributist economic system which flourished in the Catholic centuries of the past. In recent times, Archbishop Lefebvre and Bishop Fellay have specifically advocated the formation of such vocational organizations among the traditional Catholic faithful. By their very nature, guilds demand a labor force divided according to certain specialties. For our purposes, since we are dealing with a relatively small labor pool, we ought to establish guilds each dedicated to the satisfaction of one of the basic needs mentioned earlier (i.e., food, housing, clothing, and medical care). Since these guilds will be corporate bodies, uniting all the members of a certain type of trade, these bodies will need to be animated by spiritual souls. The first need for such an organization of workers is the spiritual and moral care of a chaplain. The chaplain's role would be to orient properly the minds of the "brothers" so that in their dealings with one another and their clients, they will properly implement the teachings of the Church in their own specific field of labor, along with insuring that the men are always understanding their work and their labor as a guild from the perspective of the Faith and of the ultimate goal of human life. Also, in the great spirit of the medieval guilds, a special devotion to a patron saint should bind together the Catholic life of each specific body: St. Raphael for the medical workers and St. Joseph for the construction workers readily come to mind. By giving work a Catholic spirit, and by working with those who have the same faith and who struggle to lead the same moral life, there will inevitably be a greater integration of faith and labor which will make for a more integral Catholicism on the part of those who attain membership in the guild.

Along with integrating faith and work, the system of guilds would help gain economic clout for the guild as a body of workers or professionals. Either the guild as a whole, for instance, the construction worker's guild, would be in a better bargaining position as regards specific contracts because they have an assembled team with a certain reputation in the area, or an individual employee, say a radiologist, as a member of the medical services guild would have backing him a group of professionals from the same general profession. The ultimate objective for these guilds, of course, would be to serve as the primary "organs" supplying the basic goods needed for the sustenance of the community. Not only should the work of the guilds be specifically directed to the good of their own specific communities, but the members of the communities serviced by the guilds must also take it upon themselves to support their brethren by employing them. The traditional Catholic communities must begin to employ their own people to service the primary needs of their own families. When a traditional Catholic man is looking for a wife, he, if he is sane, "looks" in specific places and among certain families. Why is it not the same when looking for an employee?

B) Guild- and Family-Owned Businesses

By organizing labor in the form of a guild system, financial resources can also be more easily pooled, making the takeover of operational businesses in the area in which most of the community lives more likely. A grocery store, farmers' co-operative, or a clothing store which has as its aim the service of the community rather than pure profit, should be a goal for the relevant guilds. It is these types of businesses, either guild or family owned, which could make the Church's demand for a just and affordable price a reality. Establishing affordable prices and providing just wages for the employees could be rendered economically feasible by a steady clientele and a high volume of sales. Business ownership also means some degree of political clout on the local level. Money means power; let us not shirk from this thought, but rather employ the truth for the financial and social well-being of our communities.

Of course, in our time, one of the fields in which we find many morally objectionable practices and attitudes is the medical field. Surely, with all the medical needs of large families, including deliveries and pre- and post-natal services, one of the goals for a medical service guild should be the establishment of a independent medical clinic or the takeover of an already operational clinic. There might even be a concerted search to find staffing for such a clinic from among traditional Catholic medical professionals looking to move to one of the various communities in the United States and elsewhere. In full accord with the "back to basics" approach of this proposal, the servicing of home-births would surely be beneficial to those large or new families seeking to avoid the astronomical price, sterility, and non-familial atmosphere of the modern hospital.

C) Homesteading

As increasing numbers of young families realize that their children need the benefits of an education at a traditional Catholic school, they will necessarily consider migrating to a traditional Catholic community which is formed around an operational educational institution, normally one which can provide an education for all the years up to and including high school. One of the concerted efforts which must be made is to provide affordable housing for these new and growing families. Affordable housing is only possible when there is affordable land upon which to put a house. It would be most probable then that the communities which could attract such new or large families would be situated in rural or semi-rural areas. In these areas, tracts of land could be bought outright, without needing to ask for the "services" of the local branch of international usury. If real property is the aim, affordable land is a necessity. The next problem to be solved is the building of affordable housing. Here I believe that the construction guild could make this their central task and "apostolate." What better way to encourage young and growing families to move to chapels which provide also a school for children, than by making affordable – really affordable – housing available to them? What better way to provide for steady and continuous work for the construction guild, than to service the demand which would no doubt exist if a ready supply were known to be available? Our slogan here should be "make work not fake work!" Of course, in these individual communities, there would need to be those who co-ordinated supply and demand. This could consist in an outreach programme attached to the construction guild. The accumulation of capital by the guild itself could facilitate the initial purchase of the tracts of land upon which the guild would build the houses, houses not generally meant for singles or for small families, but for large ones. Again, increased volume would make possible affordable prices. The goal, of course, must be to have the maximal number of families possess their own mortgage-free housing.

D) Apprenticeships

One of the aims of the proposed guild system must be the initiation of an apprenticeship system. Apprenticeships have always been the future of any guild. They have also been a source of hope for the young. The essence of the apprentice system is the existence of a master or master-craftsman and a disciple or apprentice. The relationship between master and disciple is the fundament of all true educational systems of any sort. Such a relationship, either established within a particular guild or, even, with a youth's own father serving in the role of master-craftsman, would remedy many of the dilemmas which tax the minds and hearts of our traditional Catholic youth. First, there would be a greater psychological integration. By forming fraternal bonds with the men working in the same profession who also share the same faith, the true Faith would become something more than a series of propositions learned in childhood, with little relevance to the world of work, money, and friends. Rather, by feeling himself to be a vital part of a corporate body of men united not only by a common work but by a common faith, he will not be able to help understanding the Faith to be something for mature minds. In this case, the Faith will provide him friends, mentors, customers, an occupation, hope for the future, and bread.

Second, the apprenticeship system would provide something desperately needed by our youth: a very quick transition from adolescence to adulthood. The serious work of a serious trade would not only render the youth more responsible for themselves, but it would also allow them to envision clearly the day in which they will be provident enough to form a family of their own. Attached to this idea of reviving the ancient position of the apprentice is another proposal which has a similar set of goals. It is the master/apprentice relationship applied to professional "white-collar" careers. Most of these would fall outside a guild system which has as its aim the providing of what we have called "primary goods"; if a young person should want to become a professor, lawyer, or accountant for example. For these youth, I would advance the idea of a "big brother" programme with an established network of professional contacts. These "big brothers," who are traditional Catholics who already work in the profession that the youth is trying to enter, would act as advisor, confidant, patron, and contact provider for the youth as he manoeuvres his way through the educational and professional maze that is part of the initiation into any profession. We would therefore ensure either that the communities we have been speaking of would have an entire ensemble of professionals dedicated to its service, or you would have young traditional Catholics being carefully manoeuvred into the "right" positions. We must cultivate our best and our brightest. Remember, the Masons took the idea from *us*!

E) Barter and Credit Unions

One of the most obvious problems encountered by the head of a household in his attempt to gain real property for his family is the fact that wages are not high enough to meet the demands made upon him to provide the primary goods necessary for his family's survival in our contemporary society. Our style of life cannot be maintained without going into debt to one or another of the financial institutions which, through usury and by exploiting an economic system based upon wants and whims, have gained a hold on the money supply and have somehow received "permission" to create "money," backed by nothing but the word of the institution itself. How can we avoid having the brethren go into debt? Such must be one of the primary aims of a parallel economy based upon the Distributist principles of *Rerum Novarum.* In this regard, along with the construction guild keeping prices down because of steady demand and because the objective is family sustenance and not profit, there are two other ways I would suggest for avoidance of indebtedness by our fellow co-religionists. They are a prudent and restricted use of the barter system, and the establishment of non-usurious credit unions. By the "barter system," I simply mean the exchange of service for service, rather than the exchange of service for dollar. Not only would this exchange of one man's work for another man's work further strengthen ties between man and man, family and family, but it would also allow a family to conserve whatever monetary capital it has, while absolutely avoiding the need to go to the givers of credit to pay for a service. Moreover, as far as I know, a service exchanged for service (e.g., plumbing work for chickens and eggs), would not figure as part of one's yearly income. Another way to "disinvest" legally in the System and reinvest in the homesteads of Christendom.

The other way I would propose for helping the traditional Catholic brethren to avoid the slavery of usury and, yet, to provide a source of finance for some of the projects suggested here, is to establish non-usurious credit unions. How can this be possible since the typical credit union loans out money at a lower, but still at some, rate of interest to its members? Here we must keep in mind the Catholic Church's traditional condemnation of the taking of interest on all non-profit yielding loans. Loans for housing construction are, except in cases of speculation, not profit-bearing loans. A loan with interest which serves as the initial investment money for a project which yields a profit, a *census* as the medievals would have it, was always perfectly acceptable to the Church. The loaner, in this case the proposed credit union, would simply serve as a partner in what would be a joint venture. By receiving back part of the profit from these joint ventures, the credit union, which would have to be established by the pooling of capital, would be able to loan money to those in the community who are building houses or providing for other basic and primary needs. These loans would be paid back, on schedule, without any usurious charge being attached to the loan.

F) Not Treating Brothers Like Strangers

The above proposals are based on a cold and hard fact. It is that in the near future, on the geo-political scene and on the macro-economic level, there is little hope that the ideas put forward by the Distributists in the early part of the twentieth century will be implemented. Since, however, they are part and parcel of a full Catholic vision of the rightly ordered human society and since, according to *Rerum Novarum* and *Quadragesimo Anno*, they are part of the full realization of the Social Kingship of Our Lord Jesus Christ, we must attempt to implement these ideas on the local level and the community level. We need communities for this. We have such communities established and we know of a number of other such communities, in the United States and elsewhere (Tynong, Australia, for example), which are in their nascent stage.

If we are to survive and even to prosper as communities of families animated by and adhering to Tradition, if our young are to be discouraged from going over to the other side, in their minds or in their hearts, and if we are to live the principles and doctrines that we adhere to with our minds within a hostile society, we must consider, seriously, the question, *how to do it.* The basic answer to this question is not to treat brothers like strangers.

Traditionalist Press

The true friends of the people are neither revolutionaries nor innovators: they are traditionalists. –St. Pius X

Who we are

The Traditionalist Press is a collective of Catholic laymen who are convinced that the Social Teaching of the Catholic Church provides the kernel of vital principles which can resolve the myriad problems of contemporary society: political, socio-economic and cultural. The collective believes this because the Church is the unique source of all truth, since its founder, Jesus Christ, *is* Truth.

What we do

In order to promote the Catholic view of the world, *The Traditionalist Press* publishes books and booklets; organizes conferences on subjects central to Social Teaching; and publishes a periodical, *The Traditionalist*, which seeks to educate and motivate laymen, to encourage them to take back our civilization. Our aim is to be a resource centre that aids and promotes the Catholic Renaissance that our generation so desperately needs.

For information

Contact us by e-mail at: tradpress@hotmail.com.

Or by regular mail at: The Traditionalist Press
Box 1
Moyne
County Longford
IRELAND.

Recommended Sources of Further Information

The Angelus Press

The excellent book, *The Framework of a Christian State,* by Fr. Edward Cahill, which is mentioned in the article "Two Pigs and a Cow", and *Fatherhood and Family* by the *Integrity* collective, from which the chapter "The Economics of the Catholic Family" is taken, are both available from: *The Angelus Press,* 2915 Forest Avenue, Kansas City, MO 64109, USA. Visit the website (www.angeluspress.org) or write for further information. In the latter case kindly send $1 or €1 or an International Reply Coupon (IRC) so as to cover postage.

Both books are highly recommended.

The Traditionalist

The Traditionalist is a small Catholic bulletin produced in Ireland, which concentrates on the Social Teaching of the Catholic Church. For a copy of *The Traditionalist* booklist, kindly send an IRC or one dollar/euro to our address: *The Traditionalist Press,* Box 1, County Longford, Ireland.

Triumph Communications

This is an excellent apostolate which specializes in producing audio-cassettes on a wide range of subjects of interest to all serious Catholics. Of particular interest to readers would be the two cassettes, "Catholics and Agriculture" and "The Amish Solution". For more information, kindly send an IRC or one dollar/euro to: *Triumph*

Communications, 5334 Yonge Street, Suite 2035, Toronto, Ontario M2N 6M2, Canada.

IHS Press

A publishing house dedicated solely to the propagation of Catholic Social Teaching. Currently available are: *The Outline of Sanity, Utopia of Usurers, Irish Impressions,* and *Twelve Types* by G.K. Chesterton; *The Free Press* and *The Restoration of Property* by Hilaire Belloc; *Action* by Jean Ousset; *The Church and the Land* by Fr. Vincent McNabb; *Catholicism, Protestantism, and Capitalism* by Amintore Fanfani; and *Flee to the Fields,* by the leaders of the Catholic Land Movement. For further information, visit the website (www.ihspress.com) or kindly send an IRC or one dollar/euro to: *IHS Press,* 222 W. 21st Street, Suite F-122, Norfolk, VA 23517, USA.

The Catholic Homesteading Movement

A relatively new endeavour run by Richard Fahey and his wife, who for many years have run the Christian Homesteading Movement, whilst waiting for Catholics to awaken to the call of the land. The Movement exists to help Catholics learn the basic skills necessary for life on the land. Afternoon-long, day-long, and week-long courses exist to instruct on everything from basic gardening, herbal medicines, and the essentials of homesteading to specific skills such as spinning, fruit tree grafting, oil lamp and homestead tool use. For information kindly send an ICR or one dollar/euro to the *Catholic Homesteading Movement,* 21 Delaware Square, Norwich, NY 13815, USA.